FOCUS
on Word Work

Word Work
Teacher's Guide 1

Notes and Copymasters
for Key Stage 1

Louis Fidge and
Sarah Lindsay

Collins

Published by Collins Educational
An imprint of HarperCollins*Publishers* Ltd
77–85 Fulham Palace Road
London W6 8JB

www.**Collins**Education.com
Online support for schools and colleges

© Louis Fidge and Sarah Lindsay 1998

First published 1998 as *Collins Primary Word Work*
This edition first published 2002

Reprinted 10 9 8 7 6 5 4 3 2 1

ISBN 0 00 713220 4

Louis Fidge and Sarah Lindsay assert the moral right to be identified as the authors of this work.

All rights reserved. No part of this publication may be reproduced, stored in a retrieval system, or transmitted in any form or by any other means, electronic, mechanical, photocopying, recording or otherwise, except for the pages marked *Focus on Word Work* © Louis Fidge and Sarah Lindsay, HarperCollins*Publishers* 1998, without the prior permission of the Publisher.

British Library Cataloguing in Publication Data
A catalogue record for this book is available from the British Library.

Series Editor: Janet Swarbrick
Designer: Amanda Easter
Cover design: Neil Adams
Cover photograph: Getty Images © Renee Lynn
Illustrations by Juliet Breese

Printed by Martins the Printers Ltd, Berwick

You might also like to visit
www.**fire**and**water**.com
The book lover's website

Contents

	page
Introduction	*4*
Using *Focus on Word Work*	*4*
Assessment and record keeping	*7*
***Focus on Word Work* scope and sequence (KS1)**	*10*
Teacher's notes	
Activity Book A	*11*
Activity Book B	*15*
High frequency words (Year Reception)	*19*
Activity Book C	*20*
Activity Book D	*23*
Introductory Book	*26*
High frequency words (Years 1/2)	*35*
Copymasters	*36*

Introduction

There has been much recent public debate on the teaching of reading and spelling. The National Literacy Strategy *Framework for Teaching* document contends that successful readers use as many of the following strategies as possible:

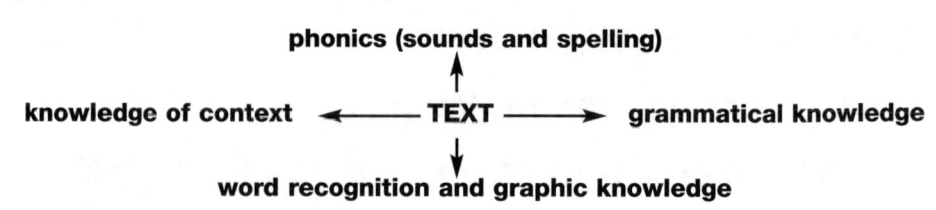

phonics (sounds and spelling)

knowledge of context ← **TEXT** → **grammatical knowledge**

word recognition and graphic knowledge

On the specific subject of phonological awareness, phonics and spelling, the document goes on to say:

> *Most teachers have been over-cautious about the teaching of phonics – sounds and spelling. It is vital that pupils are taught to use these word level strategies effectively. Research evidence shows that pupils do not learn to distinguish between the different sounds of words simply by being exposed to books. They need to be taught to do this. When they begin to read most children see words as images, with a particular shape or pattern. They tend not to understand that words are made up of letters used in particular combinations that correspond with spoken sounds. It is essential that pupils are taught these basic decoding and spelling skills from the outset.*

It suggests that:
Pupils should be taught to:
- *discriminate between the separate sounds in words;*
- *learn the letters and letter combinations most commonly used to spell those sounds;*
- *read words by sounding out and blending their separate parts;*
- *write words by combining the spelling patterns of their sounds.*

In defining a 'literate primary pupil', the National Literacy Strategy document states that literate primary pupils should 'understand the sound and spelling system and use this to read and spell accurately' and 'have an interest in words and their meanings and a growing vocabulary'.

Using Focus on Word Work

Overview

Focus on Word Work, covering ages 4 to 11, is a course designed to help schools realise the defined aims for phonological awareness, phonics and spelling in a straightforward, structured and systematic way.

Scope and sequence
Teachers should follow the progression set out in the word level objectives carefully. It sets out both an order of teaching and the expectations for what pupils should achieve by the end of each term.

The *Focus on Word Work* course follows the scope and sequence of the objectives set out in the *Framework for Teaching* document, and provides a comprehensive coverage of most of the required objectives.

At Reception this includes work on:
- phonological awareness, phonics and spelling
- word recognition, graphic knowledge and spelling
- vocabulary extension
- handwriting.

At Key Stage 1 this includes work on:
- phonological awareness, phonics and spelling
- word recognition, graphic knowledge and spelling
- vocabulary extension.

Features
- It gives pupils an opportunity to develop an understanding and competence in word level work in a developmental way, ensuring the systematic introduction, repetition and consolidation of key concepts and skills.
- It is designed to help children meet the NLS word level objectives.
- It is structured in a simple and straightforward way, allowing easy access for pupils, providing a clear focus and range of differentiated tasks.
- It provides a smooth gradient between levels of difficulty, ensuring a greater chance of success and giving pupils confidence in their growing understanding and competence.
- It ensures that the instructional language and readability level of the activities is as direct and age-appropriate as possible.
- It provides opportunities to explore tasks in a rich variety of stimulating and interesting ways, ranging from the clearly structured and directed to more open-ended activities.
- It incorporates an integrated system for regular ongoing assessment of developing skills and understanding.

Components at Reception and Key Stage 1
The *Focus on Word Work* course consists of:
1 x 128 page Teacher's Guide (including 92 copymasters for additional teaching purposes)
2 x 16 page Activity Books at Year Reception
2 x 16 page Activity Books at Year 1
1 x 48 page Introductory Book at Year 2

Focus on Word Work *and the Literacy Hour*
According to the National Literacy Strategy document, *Framework for Teaching*, word level work 'must be given a specific focus in the Literacy Hour'.
The document states, 'There must be systematic, regular and frequent teaching of phonological awareness, phonics and spelling throughout KS1.'
It also says that these decoding skills:

> ... need to be taught through carefully structured activities, which help pupils hear and discriminate regularities in speech and see how these are related to letters and letter combinations in spelling and reading. Word recognition, graphic knowledge and vocabulary work should also have a teaching focus during this period of 15 minutes.

Focus on Word Work provides an ideal way to help meet the requirements of the National Literacy Strategy word level objectives in the Literacy Hour.
- The teaching focus section in each unit provides a clear focus for introducing and discussing specific teaching points with the class as a whole.
- The three sections in each unit, 'Practice', 'More to think about' and 'Now try these', provide a range of differentiated activities to meet the needs of the whole class.
- The 'Practice' section may be undertaken as part of the class focus.
- The 'More to think about' and 'Now try these' sections may be used as a basis for class, group or individual work.

- The Teacher's Guide provides a wide range of further ideas for additional class, group and individual work, and suggestions on linking the word level work with sentence and text level reading and writing activities.
- Activities may be reviewed together, on completion, as part of the plenary session to consider common mistakes and reinforce the unit's key teaching points.
- Each course book includes progress tests which review the child's understanding of the concepts, skills and vocabulary covered in the preceding units.

The course books

Activity Books A and B for Reception and Activity Books C and D for Year 1 are divided into seven double-page teaching units and one progress test. The Introductory Book for Year 2 is divided into 20 teaching units and two progress tests.

All the books are complemented by a range of additional copymasters in the Teacher's Guide.

Each double page teaching unit is structured in a similar way:
- to facilitate planning
- to provide differentiation
- to make pages easily accessible to pupils.

The following sections appear in each unit.

Teaching focus
This section:
- introduces the key concept or skill being taught
- provides the essential vocabulary and terminology for discussion
- provides concise, clear definitions and explanations
- provides examples, always accompanied by pictorial support
- provides opportunities for whole-class teaching.

Practice
This section:
- provides activities which consolidate key points introduced in the teaching focus
- provides activities intended for all the children in the class.

More to think about
This section:
- provides an extension or a development of the main focus
- provides activities with a higher degree of difficulty, appropriate for whole class, group or individual work.

The following section appears as copymasters in the Teacher's Guide for Year R and Year 1 and in each unit in the Year 2 Introductory Book:

Now try these
This section:
- provides an extension activity, which proceeds to a third and higher level of differentiation
- is most appropriate for individual work.

The Teacher's Guide

The Teacher's Guide:
- sets the course in the context of the National Literacy Strategy
- provides information on the aims, approach, and structure of the course and practical advice on organising and using it in the Literacy Hour
- provides detailed lesson notes on each unit
- provides photocopiable class and individual record sheets
- includes a variety of additional photocopiable teaching material.

Copymasters in the Teacher's Guide

Extension copymasters for Year R and Year 1 Activity Books
One 'Now try these' copymaster is provided for each unit that extends and develops the concepts and skills introduced. This is most appropriate for individual work.

Supplementary copymasters
These occasional copymasters deal with additional spelling or phonic skill objectives not covered in the workbooks.

High frequency word copymasters
These help teach the recognition, spelling and use of the required high frequency words.

Note
Most NLS word level objectives are comprehensively covered in the course. However, there are certain objectives which were not appropriate to include as they are best addressed in the context of each individual school. These are:

	Word recognition, graphic knowledge and spelling	Vocabulary
Year R	5, 7, 8	10, 11
Year 1 Term 1	7, 8	12
Year 1 Term 2	4, 5	10
Year 1 Term 3	2, 3	8

The series does not attempt to cover handwriting, except at Reception where letter formation is included, as it appreciates that all schools have different approaches to this in terms of preferred style and the timing of the introduction of joined script.

Assessment and record keeping

Each course book includes progress tests which review the child's understanding of the concepts, skills and vocabulary covered in the preceding units. These can be used:
- to check that knowledge has been retained
- to identify areas that may need revisiting
- to provide information of individual progress
- to provide information for individual portfolios/records of achievement.

The Teacher's Guide contains both an individual and a class record sheet. These can be used to:
- check on what each child has covered
- monitor individual progress
- give an overview of the progress of the class as a whole.

Focus on Word Work: *Class Record*

Book _____ Class _____ Year _____

It is suggested that you give a brief indication of pupils' progress for each unit:
/ = attempted;   X = completed satisfactorily

Names	\multicolumn{22}{c}{Units}
	1	2	3	4	5	6	7	8	9	10	11	12	13	14	15	16	17	18	19	20	A	B

Focus on Word Work: *Individual Record*

Name _____   Book _____ Class _____ Year _____

Unit	Comment	Date
1		
2		
3		
4		
5		
6		
7		
8		
9		
10		
11		
12		
13		
14		
15		
16		
17		
18		
19		
20		
Progress Test A		
Progress Test B		

Focus on Word Work © Louis Fidge and Sarah Lindsay, HarperCollins*Publishers* 1998

Focus on Word Work *scope and sequence (KS1)*

Year Reception		Year 1		Year 2	
Activity Book A		**Activity Book C**		**Introductory Book**	
Unit	Content	Unit	Content	Unit	Content
1	*a c h t*	1	The alphabet	1	*oo* and *u*
2	*b l m s*	2	Non-rhyming words	2	Collecting words (1)
3	*g i n p*	3	Rhyming words	3	*ar*
4	*d e f r*	4	*ff ll ss*	4	Adding *ing* and *ed*
5	*k o v y*	5	*ng nk*	5	*oi* and *oy*
6	*j u w*	6	*fl tr*	6	Vowels and consonants
7	*q x z*	7	Patterns in words	7	*ow* and *ou*
	Progress Test		Progress Test	8	Antonyms
				9	*air* and *ear*
Activity Book B		**Activity Book D**		10	Compound words
					Progress Test A
Unit	Content	Unit	Content	11	*or* and *aw*
8	Capital letters	8	*nd st*	12	Collecting words (2)
9	Word building (1)	9	Plurals	13	*er*, *ir* and *ur*
10	Word families	10	*ee oo*	14	Syllables
11	Rhyming words	11	*oa ai*	15	Prefixes
12	*sh ch*	12	The word ending *ed*	16	*wh* and *ph*
13	Final letter sounds	13	The word ending *ing*	17	Collecting words (3)
14	Word building (2)	14	Vowels	18	Suffixes
	Progress Test		Progress Test	19	*ea*
				20	Synonyms
					Progress Test B

Activity Book A

Teacher's notes

Activity Book A

Unit	Content
1	a c h t
2	b l m s
3	g i n p
4	d e f r
5	k o v y
6	j u w
7	q x z
	Progress Test

Unit 1 a c h t

Objectives

2 knowledge of grapheme/phoneme correspondence through:
- hearing and identifying initial sounds in words;
- reading letters that represent sounds;
- writing each letter in response to each sound;
- identifying and writing initial . . . phonemes in spoken words;

4 to link sound and spelling patterns by:
- identifying alliteration.

Teaching focus

Introduction
NB Before attempting each unit it would be helpful for children to have done the relevant copymasters dealing with each letter sound individually, as well as having undertaken a range of other suggested activities for teaching individual letter shapes and sounds (see 'Further ideas').

These copymasters could be collated so that they gradually build up into an alphabet book of letter sounds for each child.

Using the teaching focus
Look at each picture one at a time. Read each caption to and with the children, stressing the alliterative element of each focus letter sound. Point out the focus letter in each phrase.

Think of other words beginning with the same letter sound, and make them into alliterative phrases if possible, for example 'a hairy hat'.

Ask children to repeat each phrase, stressing the focus letter sound. Encourage children to become aware of the shape of their mouths when articulating individual letter sounds, for example, put a hand in front of the mouth and feel the 'c'; notice the position of the tongue when saying 't' and so on.

Demonstrate the formation of each letter shape many times, introducing each one by writing it on the board slowly, giving a commentary as you do so, for example for the letter 't' you could say 'Start at the top, come down to the bottom and give it a flick, then go across here, like this.' (NB Always demonstrate the letter movement so children see it from the correct direction, even if this means teaching with your back to the class.)

Encourage children to write each letter in the air and on their desk tops with their fingers several times before trying it in the book.

Class and group work

Practice   This requires children to find and circle the letters being studied in a picture of the alphabet.

More to think about   Children are asked to colour the picture in each line, from a choice of three, that begins with the given letter sound, and then to draw their own pictures beginning with the letter sounds.

Now try these (Copymaster 27)   Children are asked to select the appropriate initial letter, from a choice of two, to complete each word. All the words are picture-cued. They then have to write each word at the bottom of the page.

Further ideas

General activities can be used for teaching letter shapes.
- Draw letters in the air or on table tops with fingers to get the 'feel' of them.
- Make letters out of sandpaper, or sand and glue, and finger trace them.
- Make letter shapes with Play-Doh, Plasticine and clay.
- Make letters in sand, earth or flour using a finger or stick.
- Use finger paints or paint letters using a paintbrush.
- Make body-shape letters in PE.
- Encourage children to look for, and recognise, individual letters in books and in signs around them.

General activities can be used for teaching letter sounds.
- Tongue twisters: have fun saying sentences where all the words begin with the same initial letter sound, for example, 'Peter Piper picked a peck of pickled peas.'
- Play I-spy using just a few pictures at a time and using the letter sound.
- Set up a 'letter' table which is devoted to collecting together things or pictures which begin with that letter.
- Give children two trays each labelled with a different letter. Sort a selected group of objects and pictures onto each tray according to the sound each begins with.
- Play snap with a limited number of letter shapes.
- Make some simple postboxes out of cereal packets. Label each with a different letter. Cut out pictures of things beginning with the letters chosen. Children choose the correct box in which to post each picture.

Use general activities for teaching focus letters.
- Letter 'a': cut out a big picture of an apple and stick 'a' words on it. Useful words: ambulance, ant, acrobat, apple, axe, arrow, anchor.
- Letter 'c: cut out a large cup shape. Collect 'c' pictures to stick on it. Useful words: cat, camel, caterpillar, cow, cake, candle, coat, car.
- Letter 'h': play 'Hunt the h'. Have pictures of 'h' objects scattered around the room. Children have to find as many as possible. Useful words: hair, hamster, hand, hat, horse, head, helicopter, help, hill, hop, hungry, hippo.
- Letter 't': collect 't' pictures on a large cut-out TV screen. Learn the rhyme: 'Tip-tap, tip-tap, tip-a-tap-a-tee, tip-tapping woodpecker taps on a tree'. Useful words: table, tap, teacher, teddy, telephone, television, tent, tin, tooth, torch.

Activity Book A

Unit 2 b l m s

Objectives
2 knowledge of grapheme/phoneme correspondences through:
- hearing and identifying initial sounds in words;
- reading letters that represent sounds;
- writing each letter in response to each sound;
- identifying and writing initial . . . phonemes in spoken words;

4 to link sound and spelling patterns by:
- identifying alliteration.

Teaching focus
Introduction
See the notes for Unit 1.

Using the teaching focus
See the notes for Unit 1. Adopt the same teaching procedures.

Class and group work
Practice   This requires children to find and circle the letters being studied in a picture of the alphabet.
More to think about   Children are asked to join each of the four letters to the picture that begins with its sound. They are then given instructions to colour each picture a specific colour.
Now try these (Copymaster 28)   Children are asked to select the appropriate initial letter, from a choice of two, to complete each word. All the words are picture-cued. They then have to write each word at the bottom of the page.

Further ideas
See also 'Further ideas' for teaching letter shapes and sounds in Unit 1.
- Letter 'b': children might like the tongue-twister 'Betty bought a bit of butter, but Betty's butter was very bitter'. Play the 'In my bag I have some butter (beans, bread, burgers, and so on)' game. Useful words: baby, bag, bat, bath, bike, bin, boy, bun, bus, boat.
- Letter 'l': teach the children 'Lucy Locket'. Use the phrase 'I like lots of lollies (love, lettuce, and so on)' for alliterative work. Useful words: ladder, lamp, lake, leaf, leg, lid, lion, log, lorry, lolly, letter.
- Letter 'm': have a cut-out of the moon and on it stick lots of 'm' pictures. Children can chant 'On the moon I can see a man (mouse and so on)'. Useful words: mat, man, map, mill, monkey, mountain, mouse, mirror, mug.
- Letter 's': make up silly sentences about Sam, for example 'Sam likes smelly socks'. Draw a snake outline and fill it with 's' pictures. Useful words: sack, saw, sea, sink, skirt, slide, snow, spoon, star, sweet, sausage.

Unit 3 g i n p

Objectives
2 knowledge of grapheme/phoneme correspondences through:
- hearing and identifying initial sounds in words;
- reading letters that represent sounds;
- writing each letter in response to each sound;
- identifying and writing initial . . . phonemes in spoken words;

4 to link sound and spelling patterns by:
- identifying alliteration.

Teaching focus
Introduction
See the notes for Unit 1.

Using the teaching focus
See the notes for Unit 1. Adopt the same teaching procedures.

Class and group work
Practice   This requires children to find and circle the letters being studied in a picture of the alphabet.
More to think about   Children are asked to follow a trail of tangled lines to discover which picture begins with which letter. They then have to write the correct letter under each picture and colour the pictures according to specific instructions.
Now try these (Copymaster 29)   Children are asked to select the appropriate initial letter, from a choice of two, to complete each picture-cued word. They then have to write each word at the bottom of the page.

Further ideas
See also 'Further ideas' for teaching letter shapes and sounds in Unit 1.
- Letter 'g': draw pictures to finish the sentence 'In my garden I have a gorilla (gate, guitar, and so on)'. Useful words: garage, garden, gate, ghost, girl, goal, gold, gorilla, glass, gloves.
- Letter 'i': say these for fun, 'Drinking ink makes me ill'; 'Eating insects makes me ill too!' Useful words: (few words begin with 'i') ink, ill, insects, invitation.
- Letter 'n': play 'The Farmer's in his Den' saying 'The farmer needs a nurse (nail, newspaper, and so on)'. Useful words: name, neck, nest, nail, nose, number, nut, needle, night, nine.
- Letter 'p': teach the tongue-twister 'Peter Piper picked a peck of pickled peppers'. Put 'p' objects on a plate. Useful words: paint, pan, peg, pen, pencil, picnic, plug, pyjamas, plums, potato, pear, pizza.

Activity Book A

Unit 4 d e f r

Objectives

2 knowledge of grapheme/phoneme correspondences through:
- hearing and identifying initial sounds in words;
- reading letters that represent sounds;
- writing each letter in response to each sound;
- identifying and writing initial . . . phonemes in spoken words;

4 to link sound and spelling patterns by:
- identifying alliteration.

Teaching focus

Introduction
See the notes for Unit 1.

Using the teaching focus
See the notes for Unit 1. Adopt the same teaching procedures.

Class and group work

Practice This requires children to find and circle the letters being studied in a picture of the alphabet.

More to think about Children are asked to colour the picture in each line, from a choice of three, that begins with the given letter sound, and then to draw their own pictures beginning with the letter sounds.

Now try these (Copymaster 30) Children are asked to select the appropriate initial letter, from a choice of two, to complete each picture-cued word. They then have to write each word at the bottom of the page.

Further ideas

See also 'Further ideas' for teaching letter shapes and sounds in Unit 1.
- Letter 'd': play an action game. Give simple instructions like 'Show me how you . . . dig'. Children mime the actions. Use verbs like dance, draw, dive, drive, drink, dust, disappear, and so on. Useful words: deer, dinosaur, donkey, dentist, dinner, doll, door, doctor, duck.
- Letter 'e': make silly sentences about elephants, for example 'Elephants like eggs'. Useful words: elephant, egg, envelope, elbow, exit, escalator.
- Letter 'f': adapt the rhyme 'Five Fat Sausages', for example 'Five fish fingers fizzling in a pan, fizzle, fizzle, fizzle, one went bang!' Draw a large outline feather on which to fix 'f' pictures. Useful words: fan, farm, feather, foot, fish, flag, fox, fork, frog, face, fire, fridge.
- Letter 'r': have fun with the 'Round and round the rugged rock the ragged rascal ran' tongue twister. Useful words: rain, rag, rake, run, rattle, read, ring, rock, rocket, rug, rope.

Unit 5 k o v y

Objectives

2 knowledge of grapheme/phoneme correspondences through:
- hearing and identifying initial sounds in words;
- reading letters that represent sounds;
- writing each letter in response to each sound;
- identifying and writing initial . . . phonemes in spoken words;

4 to link sound and spelling patterns by:
- identifying alliteration.

Teaching focus

Introduction
See the notes for Unit 1.

Using the teaching focus
See the notes for Unit 1. Adopt the same teaching procedures.

Class and group work

Practice This requires children to find and circle the letters being studied in a picture of the alphabet.

More to think about Children are asked to join each of the four letters to the picture that begins with its sound. They are then given instructions to colour each picture a specific colour.

Now try these (Copymaster 31) Children are asked to select the appropriate initial letter, from a choice of two, to complete each picture-cued word. They then have to write each word at the bottom of the page.

Further ideas

See also 'Further ideas' for teaching letter shapes and sounds in Unit 1.
- Letter 'k': have a flying kite with 'k' pictures stuck on it. Useful words: kangaroo, koala, king, kitchen, kettle, kennel, kitten, kilt, key.
- Letter 'o': Learn a silly sentence like 'Olly the odd octopus likes oranges and ostriches!' Useful words: octopus, ostrich, orange, ox, odd.
- Letter 'v': have a cut-out picture of a van. Play the 'Into the van I can put a vase (vest, violin, and so on)' game. Useful words: van, vet, vulture, vest, volcano, vase, video, village, violin, vinegar.
- Letter 'y': have pictures of yellow 'y' things. Useful words: yak, yo-yo, yoghurt, yacht.

Unit 6 j u w

Objectives

2 knowledge of grapheme/phoneme correspondences through:
- hearing and identifying initial sounds in words;
- reading letters that represent sounds;
- writing each letter in response to each sound
- identifying and writing initial . . . phonemes in spoken words;

4 to link sound and spelling patterns by:
- identifying alliteration.

Teaching focus

Introduction
See the notes for Unit 1.

Using the teaching focus
See the notes for Unit 1. Adopt the same teaching procedures.

Class and group work

Practice This requires children to find and circle the letters being studied in a picture of the alphabet.

13

Activity Book A

More to think about   Children are asked to follow a trail of tangled lines to discover which picture begins with which letter. They then have to write the correct letter under each picture and colour the pictures according to specific instructions.

Now try these (Copymaster 32)   Children are asked to select the appropriate initial letter, from a choice of two, to complete each picture-cued word. They then have to write each word at the bottom of the page.

Further ideas

See also 'Further ideas' for teaching letter shapes and sounds in Unit 1.
- Letter 'j': make a jam jar collection of 'j' pictures in a large cut out jam jar. Useful words: jaws, jacket, jeans, jigsaw, jug, juggler, juice, jelly, jack-in-a-box.
- Letter 'u': learn a silly sentence like 'I'm unhappy under my ugly umbrella in my underwear'. Useful words: up, umbrella, unhappy, underwear, ugly, under.
- Letter 'w': invite children to think of 'w' words to complete 'I wish I was a walrus (worm, and so on)'. Learn to say: 'Wiggle, waggle, woggle, went the wiggly worm'. Useful words: waiter, walrus, wasp, weasel, whale, wizard, wolf, worm, wall, watch.

Unit 7   q x z

Objectives

2   knowledge of grapheme/phoneme correspondences through:
- hearing and identifying initial sounds in words;
- reading letters that represent sounds;
- writing each letter in response to each sound;
- identifying and writing initial (and final) . . . phonemes in spoken words;

4   to link sound and spelling patterns by:
- identifying alliteration.

Teaching focus

Introduction

See the notes for Unit 1.

Using the teaching focus

See the notes for Unit 1. Adopt the same teaching procedures.

Class and group work

Practice   This requires children to find and circle the letters being studied in a picture of the alphabet.

More to think about   Children are asked to colour the picture in each line, from a choice of three, that begins with the given letter sound – 'q' or 'z'. They are then asked to find and colour the picture that ends with an 'x'.

Now try these (Copymaster 33)   Children are asked to select the appropriate initial letter, from a choice of two, or final letter in the case of 'x', to complete each picture-cued word. They then have to write each word at the bottom of the page.

Further ideas

See also 'Further ideas' for teaching letter shapes and sounds in Unit 1.
- Letter 'q': invite children to think of 'q' words to complete 'The queen likes quince (questions, and so on)'. Useful words: quack, quince queue, quilt, queen, question, quarter, quarrel, quill.
- Letter 'x': remind children that 'X' stands for kiss! It sounds like kiss without the 'i'! Have an 'X marks the spot', in a sand tray. Under the 'X' put some words ending in 'x'. Useful words: fix, mix, six, box, fox, fax, ox.
- Letter 'z': children pretend to be bees buzzing through the air! Useful words: zebra, zigzag, zip, zoo, zap.

Activity Book B

Unit	Content
8	Capital letters
9	Word building (1)
10	Word families
11	Rhyming words
12	sh ch
13	Final letter sounds
14	Word building (2)
	Progress Test

Unit 8 Capital letters

Objectives
3 alphabetic and phonic knowledge through:
- sounding and naming each letter of the alphabet in lower and upper case;
- writing letters in response to letter names;
- understanding alphabetical order.

Teaching focus
Introduction
Remind children where they will have seen capital letters used in a variety of situations – at the beginning of their names, in books, on alphabet friezes, on signs around them and so on.

Explain that all the letters of the alphabet can be written in two ways, and that each letter can have a sound and a name. Just like a dog, it makes a sound – it barks, and has a name – a dog!

By reference to the children's badges (see 'Further ideas'), draw attention to the fact that these 'big' letters, the capital letters, are often a different shape from the smaller, lower case, letters.

Explain that capital letters are used in special words, for example people's names, names of places, days of the week, months of the year, and so on, and that we usually write in smaller, lower case, letters most of the time.

Using the teaching focus
NB It it best to spread the teaching focus and 'Practice' sections over a period of time, rather than trying to do them at one go.

Look at the alphabet. Sing the letters of 'the alphabet song' to and with the children, several times, to the tune of 'Twinkle, Twinkle Little Star', pointing to each letter, one at a time as you do so.

Identify the capital letters whose lower case letters are the same shape.

Point out that capital letters always sit on the line when we write them. If possible, have the capital letter alphabet displayed in alphabetical order around the room.

Children can play 'the matching game'. Give them a different lower case letter to match to its capital, repeating both the name and the sound of each letter as it is done.

Demonstrate the formation of each capital letter shape many times, introducing each one by writing it on the board slowly, giving a commentary as you do so. (NB Always demonstrate the letter movement so children see it from the correct direction, even if this means teaching with your back to the class.) This is best done over a period of time.

Encourage children to write each letter in the air and on their desk tops with their fingers several times before trying it in the book.

The 'Practice' section is, therefore, also best spread over a period of days, rather than being tried all at once.

Class and group work
Practice   Children are given the alphabet written in capital letters, in dotted letters, each with a starting dot and directional arrow.

More to think about   This page consists of a 'photo' gallery of children. Each picture has the child's name under it, with the initial letter missing. The pictures are arranged in alphabetical order.

Now try these (Copymaster 34)   Children are given letters of the alphabet, in both upper and lower case. The task for the child is to supply the missing upper or lower case letters.

Further ideas
- Make badges for each child.
- Sing 'the alphabet song' (see 'Using the teaching focus') daily, always pointing to each letter in turn.
- Play 'the matching game' (see 'Using the teaching focus') regularly.
- Make some 'alphabet snap' cards of both upper and lower case letters. Use just a few at a time and gradually increase the number being played with.
- Make 'alphabet books' and collect pictures for each letter. The individual copymasters 1–26 can form the basis of these.
- Look for capital letters in books and signs around the classroom and school.

Unit 9 Word building (1)

NB Many of the activities in the rest of the workbook depend on children manipulating letter sounds and word building. The work in the workbooks is best supported by a wide range of opportunities for children to handle letters in a concrete way and experiment with them. Individual letter cards, with and without picture cues, magnetic letters, wooden or plastic letters, and so on are all helpful.

Objectives
2 knowledge of grapheme/phoneme correspondences through:
- identifying and writing initial phonemes in consonant-vowel-consonant (CVC) words;

4 to link sound and spelling patterns by:
- discriminating 'onsets' from 'rimes' in speech and spelling.

Teaching focus
Introduction
Once children recognise individual letter sounds and associate them with letter shapes they can learn how letters can be joined together to make simple CVC words. The approach taken in this book is to focus on initial letters (onsets) and the rest of the single-syllable words, like 'at' and 'og' (rimes).

The word building activities involve experimenting with putting initial letter sounds with rimes to make new words. Such activities lead to the recognition of commonly recurring letter strings.

Activity Book B

Using the teaching focus
Have some large cards with each onset and rime featured, for demonstrating the process. Look at, and name, the picture of the cat. Hold up the 'c' card with your left hand and the 'at' card with your right hand. Discuss how 'a' and 't' together make the rime 'at'. Then gradually move the two cards together, saying 'c' and 'at', as you do so until they make and say the word 'cat', showing how the onset and rime can be joined to make the word. Repeat this with 'hat'. Ask the children for other rhyming 'at' words, for example 'bat', 'fat', 'mat', 'pat', 'rat', 'sat'. These could also be word-built in the same way if desired. Repeat the same process with the 'og' words.

Class and group work
Practice Children are asked to fit together the onset and rime elements of words, and write the words they make. The words are arranged into two sets – 'at' and 'og' words. All words are picture-cued.
More to think about Children are given a set of six pictures (CVC words) and the rime element of each. They are asked to choose the correct initial letter, from a choice of two, to complete each word.
Now try these (Copymaster 35) Children are given the onsets and rime elements of words to build. They then have to match the words with pictures. The words are arranged into two families – 'an' and 'in' words.

Further ideas
- Undertake a lot of oral rhyming activities to help children 'tune in' and become aware that sound is a significant element in words.
- Look for, and read, a wide range of books containing phonically regular onset and rime elements, for example *Dr Seuss* books, drawing attention to the significant features of the words.
- Provide children with rime cards containing a vowel and a consonant, and encourage them to try to make up words by experimenting with adding different initial letters.
- Useful rimes: ab, ad, ag, am, an, ap, at; ed, eg, em, en, et; ib, id, ig, im, in, ip, it, ix; ob, od, og, om, on, op, ot, ox; ub, ud, ug, um, un, up, ut.

Unit 10   Word families

Objectives
1   to understand and be able to rhyme through:
- recognising, exploring and working with rhyming patterns;

2   knowledge of grapheme/phoneme correspondences through:
- identifying and writing . . . dominant phonemes in CVC words;

4   to link sound and spelling patterns by:
- using knowledge of rhyme to identify families of rhyming CVC words;
- discriminating 'onsets' from 'rimes' in speech and spelling;

9   to recognise the critical features of words, for example . . . common spelling patterns.

Teaching focus
Introduction
An important element of learning to spell is the ability to recognise letter patterns. In the early stages both the auditory (rhyming) and visual elements are very important. This work on word families helps focus on both aspects.

Using the teaching focus
Discuss how members of families often have a similar appearance in some ways. Explain that it is possible to put words into word families by their appearance and the sounds they make.

Look at, and read, the 'eg' words, ensuring the children understand the meaning of each word.

The words can then be word-built as described in Unit 9.

Draw attention to the common rhyming sound they share. Ask children what they notice about the way the three words look.

Draw attention to the common letter pattern they each have.

Follow the same procedure for dealing with the 'ot' words.

Class and group work
Practice Children are given a set of eight words in the form of stepping stones. They have to find and colour the four 'ip' and the four 'an' words by looking carefully.
More to think about There are nine balloons with CVC words in and three children. The balloons have to be joined to the correct child, according to their rime element. The words then have to be written in their three separate 'families'.
Now try these (Copymaster 36) Children are given sets of four CVC words, one of which does not belong. This has to be identified. Children then write the words in word family groups.

Further ideas
- Make 'family albums' of CVC words, grouped according to letter and rime patterns.
- Give children a limited number of CVC words to be sorted into families. Begin with just two families and gradually increase the number.
- This could also be a colouring activity along the lines of the 'practice' activity.
- Play 'Happy Families' with word cards.
- Play 'Find the Stranger'. Give children sets of words, each set containing a word that does not belong.

Unit 11   Rhyming words

Objectives
1   to understand and be able to rhyme through:
- recognising, exploring and working with rhyming patterns;
- extending these patterns by analogy. . . ;

2   knowledge of grapheme/phoneme correspondences through:
- identifying and writing . . . dominant phonemes in CVC words;

4   to link sound and spelling patterns by:
- using knowledge of rhyme to identify families of rhyming CVC words;
- discriminating 'onsets' from 'rimes' in speech and spelling;

9   to recognise the critical features of words, for example . . . common spelling patterns.

Activity Book B

Teaching focus
Introduction
The auditory input, the ability to distinguish and differentiate sounds, is very important in the development of phonic skills. Rhyming is an ideal way of focusing on this. It helps tune children's ears to patterns of sound and establish the link between sounds and letter patterns in words.

Initially, only phonically regular rimes, where sound and letter patterns correspond, are used in this book for teaching purposes. Later, of course, children will learn that many rhyming words do not share a common spelling pattern.

Using the teaching focus
The focus consists of three rhyming couplets from well-known nursery rhymes. Introduce 'Jack and Jill' by asking children who know the rhyme to say it.

Repeat the rhyme, emphasising the rhyming words, and ask children to say what they notice.
Use the word 'rhyme' as a descriptor. Look at the rhyming couplet on the page and draw attention to the look and the sound of the pair of rhyming words.

Repeat the process with the other two examples.

Class and group work
Practice Children have to join up the pairs of matching CVC words from two sets of six words. Ensure they can read the words.
More to think about Children are given two pictures with captions of rhyming words and asked to make simple rhymes with them to go with a third picture, for example 'a hat on a cat'.
Now try these (Copymaster 37) Children are given pictures and an accompanying rhyming sentence with the key rhyming words omitted. The missing rhyming words are given and children have to choose the best word to go in each gap to complete each sentence.

Further ideas
- Play a range of listening games. Blindfold children and ask them to identify common sounds.
- Sing nursery rhymes and other simple rhymes together.
- Play silly games with children by giving them 'wrong' rhymes and asking them to spot the mistake, for example 'Humpty Dumpty sat on the wall, Humpty Dumpty had a great . . . sit'.
- Share rhyming stories, such as the *Dr Seuss* books, and nursery rhyme books together. Encourage children to join in with them.
- Make up silly rhymes together, for example 'When the dog carried the bag, it made his tail . . .'

Unit 12 sh ch

Objectives
2 knowledge of grapheme/phoneme correspondences through:
- reading letters that represent the sounds 'sh' and 'ch';
- writing each letter in response to each sound 'sh' and 'ch';
- identifying and writing initial and dominant phonemes in spoken words;

4 to link sound and spelling patterns by:
- discriminating 'onsets' from 'rimes' in speech and spelling.

Teaching focus
Introduction
The 'sh' and 'ch' digraphs are very common in high frequency words. As well as learning that letters linked together individually make words, children gradually need to learn that letters can join together to produce new sounds. Children need to learn that these combinations, when they occur, are not sounded separately, but as one unit of sound.

Using the teaching focus
Have two cards, one with 's' and one with 'h' on. Hold them up one at a time and ask children the sound of each letter.

Write the word 'ship' on the board and tell them what it says. Ask them what they notice about the 's' and 'h'. Hold the 's' and 'h' cards up and bring them together. Physically join the two cards in some way, for example with sticky tape. Say the sound the letters make together. Put your finger against your lips as in a 'shushing', 'be quiet' gesture to help children remember.

Explain that whenever the two letters come together they always make this new sound.

Repeat the process with the 'ch' digraph, likening it to the sound of a sneeze, or the sound of a train chugging along.

Then read and study together the phrases in the teaching focus section.

Class and group work
Practice Children are given a set of 'sh' and 'ch' pictures. They have to copy the words correctly and colour the pictures according to specific instructions.
More to think about Children are asked to build words beginning with 'sh' and 'ch'. They then colour the accompanying pictures according to specific instructions.
Now try these (Copymaster 38) Children are given six pictures, under which are words with the 'sh' and 'ch' missing in both initial and final positions. Children have to select the correct letters to complete each word, and then to write the whole words again at the bottom of the page.

Further ideas
- Some useful 'sh' words: shed, shop, shin, ship, shut, shot; fish, dish, wish, cash, bash, mash, dash, rush, hush, gush.
- Some useful 'ch' words: chin, chip, chop, chap, chat, chum; rich, much, such.
- Have fun making up alliterative sentences containing 'sh' or 'ch' words. As these are for listening to and saying, not for writing, the way the words are written is not important, for example 'The shy sheep went to the fish shop'; 'The cheeky chimp ate a bar of chocolate'.
- Let the children find examples of 'sh' and 'ch' words in reading books.
- Provide the children with more activities like those in the workbook and on the copymaster, focusing on 'sh' and 'ch'.
- Copymaster 41 introduces the 'th' digraph.

Activity Book B

Unit 13 Final letter sounds

Objectives
2 knowledge of grapheme/phoneme correspondences through:
- identifying and writing initial and dominant phonemes in spoken words;
- identifying and writing initial and final phonemes in consonant-vowel-consonant (CVC) words.

Teaching focus
Introduction
Spelling involves the gradual refinement and development of children's auditory and visual skills. Individual letter sounds are normally taught as initial letters of words. It is important to encourage children to distinguish these at the end of phonically regular CVC words also. (NB Only the letters 'b', 'd', 'g', 'm', 'n', 'p', 't' and 'x' regularly occur at the end of such words.)

Using the teaching focus
The teaching focus introduces identifying final letters in a humorous way: the children word-build the two words 'cap' and 'cat' by synthesising the letters and deciding which of the two endings is required.

Have two cards, one with the word 'cat' and one with the word 'cap' on. Hold them both up together and encourage children to read each, stressing the final sound.

Play a game, putting the cards behind your back and holding one card up at random, and ask children to decide which word it is by focusing on the final letter.

Look at the two sentences and illustrations on the page to bring home the importance of paying attention to the final letter sounds!

Class and group work
Practice Six pictures are provided with CVC words written underneath. Children have to identify and colour those which end with a 't'.

More to think about Nine pictures with CVC words written underneath are supplied. Children have to decide if the word is correct or not depending on the final letter sound in each case.

Now try these (Copymaster 39) Children are given nine pictures, each with the appropriate CVC word written underneath, except for the final letter. Children have to select the correct letter, from a choice of two, to complete each word.

Further ideas
- Give children a range of consonant and vowel word beginnings, for example 'ca', 'de', 'pi', 'fo', 'pu', and final letter cards 'b', 'd', 'g', 'm', 'n', 'p', 't', 'x'. See how many different words they can make.
- Play auditory discrimination games. Have a set of pictures and ask children to decide which of two words, with only the final letter different in each, for example, 'cut', 'cup', matches each picture.
- Provide children with more activities along the lines of those in the workbook and copymaster.

Unit 14 Word building (2)

Objectives
2 knowledge of grapheme/phoneme correspondences through:
- identifying and writing initial . . . phonemes in consonant-vowel-consonant (CVC) words;

4 to link sound and spelling patterns by:
- discriminating 'onsets' from 'rimes' in speech and spelling.

Teaching focus
Introduction
This unit builds on and develops the work covered in Unit 9. It covers the same sort of skills and introduces a few consonant blends as onsets as well as individual letter onsets.

Using the teaching focus
Have three large cards with 't', 'r' and 'ip' on respectively. Look at the picture of the rip and discuss it. Hold up the 'r' card with your left hand and the 'ip' card with your right hand. Discuss how 'i' and 'p' together make the rime 'ip'. Then gradually move the two cards together, saying both 'r' and 'ip' as you do so until they make and say the word 'rip', showing how the onset and rime can be joined to make the word.

Now look at the picture of the trip. Say the word and draw attention to the fact that it rhymes and ends in the same way, with 'ip'.

Hold up the 't' and 'r' cards and ask children for the sound of each letter. Draw them together and note how together they make the 'tr' sound. Physically join the cards to make one card, and one sound, with sticky tape.

Demonstrate how, by joining 'tr' and 'ip', the word 'trip' can be built.

Repeat this process with the words 'sip' and 'skip'.

Class and group work
Practice Children are asked to fit together the onset and rime elements of words and write the words they make. The words are arranged into three sets – 'ap', 'in' and 'od' words.

More to think about: Children are given a set of six pictures with simple, phonically regular three or four letter words and the rime element of each. They are asked to choose the correct initial letter or letters (from a choice of two) to complete each word.

Now try these (Copymaster 40) Children are given the onsets and rime elements of words to build. They then have to match the words with pictures. The words are arranged into two families – 'ill' and 'ick' words.

Further ideas
- Look for, and read, a wide range of books containing phonically regular onset and rime elements, for example *Dr Seuss* books, drawing attention to the significant features of the words.
- Provide children with rime cards containing vowel and consonant, and encourage them to try to make up words by experimenting with adding different initial letters, and different consonant blends, for example various consonant plus 'l' ('bl', 'cl', 'fl', and so on), consonant plus 'r' ('br', 'cr', 'dr', and so on), or 's' plus consonant ('sk', 'sp', and so on) blends.
- Useful rimes: ab, ad, ag, am, an, ap, at; ed, eg, em, en, et; ib, id, ig, im, in, ip, it, ix; ob, od, og, om, on, op, ot, ox; ub, ud, ug, um, un, up, ut.

High frequency words (Year Reception)

Objectives
6 to read on sight the 45 high frequency words to be taught by the end of Year R;
9 to recognise the critical features of words.

Copymaster 42: Year R High frequency words checklist

This may be used for a variety of purposes.
1 It may be given to children:
 - to be stuck onto card. The words may be cut out and used as flash cards for learning on sight or for making sentences or phrases with;
 - to be stuck onto card. The words may be cut out and used in a variety of games, for example snap, Pelmanism, the high frequency words game (see below), or the fishing game. To make the fishing game put a paper clip on each word card and make a simple rod and line with a magnet on the end. Put the 'fish' into a box. Let the children fish the words out one at a time and keep each word they know. They see how many 'fish' they can catch;
 - to be used as a record sheet by each child to colour as words are learnt and remembered.
2 It may be used by the teacher:
 - as a prompt or test card to show children to check which words they know;
 - as an individual record sheet for each child;
 - to be pasted on card and used as the caller's cards in word lotto games, and as the caller's check-up card to keep a note of which words have been called during the course of a game.

Copymasters 43–46: High frequency words lotto cards

These may be stuck onto card, cut out and used as lotto cards by children. There are 12 separate cards each containing 15 of the 45 high frequency words in different combinations, encouraging word recognition.

Copymaster 47: High frequency words game

This is a game for two to four children who need a dice and a counter each and a set of high frequency word cards placed face down on the desk. Children take turns to throw the dice. They must turn over the card from the top of the pile and read the high frequency word before they can move their counter the number shown on the dice. If they cannot read the word, they cannot move their counter. The high frequency word is put on one side and the next child throws the dice and repeats the above. The winner is the first child to reach the end of the course. This game encourages word recognition.

Copymasters 48–50: Using high frequency words

These sheets provide open-ended activities encouraging children to compose sentences involving the use of a selection of high frequency words.

Copymasters 51–53: Writing high frequency words

These copymasters encourage children to look carefully at a selection of high frequency words, noticing especially their shape, length and spelling.

Activity Book C

Activity Book C

Unit	Content
1	The alphabet
2	Non-rhyming words
3	Rhyming words
4	ff ll ss
5	ng nk
6	fl tr
7	Patterns in words
	Progress Test

Unit 1   The alphabet

Objectives
T1 **2**   from Year R to practise and secure alphabetic letter knowledge and alphabetic order.

Teaching focus
Introduction
This unit enables the child to consolidate and revise work undertaken in Year R. It assumes basic knowledge of the alphabet.

Using the teaching focus
Begin by reading or singing the alphabet to and with the class several times, focusing on both the sounds and the letters.

Encourage children to follow the directional arrows on the letters of the alphabet using just a finger.

When they appear ready ask them to write over each letter.
Discuss with the children for which letters the pencil needs to come off the page and for which letters the pencil must stay down.

Class and group work
Practice   This exercise establishes the alphabet in its order. Reference can be made to the fact that the five letters missing are the vowel letters.
More to think about   Half crackers are labelled with letters from the alphabet. Children join the two letters that lie next to each other in the alphabet.
Now try these (Copymaster 54)   Children are asked to focus on the first letter in each word. Then they write two words in the order they would be found in the alphabet.

Further ideas
- Look at the creatures named and pictured (a hen and a bat) in the unit. Discuss with the children which letter each creature begins with. Ask them which letter the other creature pictured (the dog) begins with. Then ask them to think of other creatures and say which letter each begins with.
- Children could do a similar exercise to the 'Now try these' but using children's names.
- Make a class alphabet frieze.
- Introduce children to a simple dictionary, making the connection with their word books.
- Display and discuss other books that are organised by alphabetical order, for example telephone books.

Unit 2   Non-rhyming words

Objectives
T1 **3**   from Year R to practise and secure the ability to hear initial and final phonemes in CVC words;
T1 **4**   to discriminate and segment all three phonemes in CVC words;
T1 **5**   to blend phonemes to read CVC words in . . . non-rhyming sets;
T1 **6**   to represent in writing the three phonemes in CVC words, spelling them . . . in non-rhyming sets;
T2 **1**   to secure identification, spelling and reading of initial, final and medial letter sounds in simple words.

Teaching focus
Introduction
Although this unit concentrates on non-rhyming words, all words in a group are linked because they start with the same initial phoneme – the smallest unit of sound in a word. All words in the unit have the CVC letter pattern.

Using the teaching focus
Initially the words are broken down, aiding the child in recognising the different sounds that make up the word. Children should be encouraged to read the words aloud.

Class and group work
Practice   Children fill in the missing letter in each word. All the words start with the letter 'b'.
More to think about   Children are provided with four sets of two words, and their illustrations. A third word that begins with the same letter has to be found in each set and its picture drawn.
Now try these (Copymaster 55)   This puzzle asks the children to choose one letter from each column to make the three-letter word that matches the picture.

Further ideas
- Verbal and written games can be played, giving children a letter from the alphabet and asking them to think of three-letter words beginning with that letter.
- The same can be done but asking them to think of three-letter words ending with that letter.
- Ask children to look in their reading books and find as many three-letter words as they can, then ask them to arrange the words according to their initial letters.

Unit 3   Rhyming words

Objectives
T1 **1**   from Year R to practise and secure the ability to rhyme, and to relate this to spelling patterns through:
- exploring and playing with rhyming patterns;
- generating rhyming strings;

T1 **3**   from Year R to practise and secure the ability to hear initial and final phonemes in CVC words;
T1 **4**   to discriminate and segment all three phonemes in CVC words;
T1 **5**   to blend phonemes to read CVC words in rhyming . . . sets;
T1 **6**   to represent in writing the three phonemes in CVC words, spelling them first in rhyming sets;
T2 **1**   to secure identification, spelling and reading of initial, final and medial letter sounds in simple words.

Activity Book C

Teaching focus

Introduction
When working with rhyming words it is very important to point out the visual as well as the auditory patterns in the words.

Using the teaching focus
Ask the children to say the words aloud.

Say a few nursery rhymes with the children, emphasising the rhyming words. Ask them if they can see the pattern.

Ask them to think of more 'at' words.

Class and group work

Practice This exercise asks children to find a word that rhymes with the key word. The words are picture-cued.
More to think about In these sets of words, one word does not rhyme with the key word in each set. Children are asked to circle the odd word out in each set.
Now try these (Copymaster 56) Children are given pictures and are asked to write the words these pictures represent into the table, organising the words into their rhyming families.

Further ideas

- This unit could be an introduction to text level work on rhymes with predictable and repeating patterns. Children can be encouraged to extend and invent patterns in rhyme.
- Play rhyme cloze activities, for example ask for a silly rhyming word in familiar verses such as 'Jack and Jill went up the pill'.
- Ask the children which two words rhyme in a familiar nursery rhyme, and so on.

Unit 4 ff ll ss

Objectives

T2 **2** to investigate, read and spell words ending in 'ff', 'll', 'ss' . . .

Teaching focus

Introduction
Usually double letter patterns are found only at the end of short phonically regular words, after a single vowel.

Using the teaching focus
It is important that children recognise the double letters at the end of the words. It may help them to write out the double letters a few times to focus their thoughts.

Brainstorm other double letter pattern words with the children and list them on the board.

Class and group work

Practice Choosing from the patterns 'ff', 'll' and 'ss', children are asked to complete and then write the correct word for the picture.
More to think about Words ending in the double letters 'ff', 'll' or 'ss' are given. The words are to be sorted by their endings into the table.
Now try these (Copymaster 57) Words with 'ff', 'll' and 'ss' endings are provided. The most suitable word in each of the sentences needs to be written. Picture-cues for each sentence are provided.

Further ideas

- Ask the children to build sentences of their own, first using one double letter word in a sentence, then two, and possibly three.
- Challenge children to find as many 'ff', 'll' or 'ss' words as possible.
- Link double letter pattern words with rhyming activities.
- Useful words: fill, mill, pill, Jill; doll, roll; puff, gruff, stuff; stiff; kiss, miss, hiss; fuss; loss, moss, boss.

Unit 5 ng nk

Objectives

T2 **2** to investigate, read and spell words ending in . . . ('ck'), 'ng'.

Teaching focus

Introduction
This unit introduces words ending in 'ng' and 'nk'. These letter pairs make single consonant sounds.

Using the teaching focus
Encourage children to say the words aloud, with emphasis on the final sound.

Ask them to write the 'ng' and 'nk' letters a number of times to reinforce the focus of the unit.

Class and group work

Practice Choosing from the patterns 'ng' and 'nk', children are asked to complete words and then write the word. Picture cues are provided.
More to think about Words ending in 'ng' and 'nk' are given. Children sort the words by their endings into the table.
Now try these (Copymaster 58) Word beginnings, each with a picture-cue, are given. Children find the correct ending, 'ng' or 'nk', to the word beginning that labels the picture. They are then asked to write more words with 'ng' and 'nk' endings.

Further ideas

- Additional work covering 'ck' can be found on Copymaster 68.
- Children can look for other examples of 'ng' and 'nk' words in stories and poems.
- Many 'ng' and 'nk' words are onomatopoeic. This can be a good link with work on descriptive writing or captions to short cartoons.
- Children can compose their own sentences using words they have found ending in 'ng' and 'nk'.

Unit 6 fl tr

Objectives

T2 **3** To discriminate, read and spell words with initial consonant clusters:
- to identify separate phonemes within words containing clusters in speech and writing;
- to blend phonemes in words with clusters for reading;
- to segment clusters into phonemes for spelling.

21

Activity Book C

Teaching focus
Introduction
In a consonant cluster the two or more letter sounds that run together are pronounced, unlike a digraph that makes a single sound. These initial consonant clusters are an ideal opportunity to practise onset and rime.

Using the teaching focus
Again, encourage children to say the words aloud, focusing on the initial 'fl' and 'tr' sound.

Ask them to write the letter cluster a number of times to reinforce the focus of the unit.

Class and group work
Practice   Children add the initial consonant cluster 'fl' and 'tr' sounds to the provided word endings, then write the word. Pictures cues are provided.
More to think about   Words beginning with 'fl' or 'tr' are given. Children sort the words by their initial consonant clusters into the table.
Now try these (Copymaster 59)   The initial consonant clusters 'fl' and 'tr' and different word endings are given. Children write the words that can be made when the endings are added to the initial consonant clusters. They also write another word beginning with 'fl' and one with 'tr'.

Further ideas
- Make the 'Now try these' activity into a card game. Use other initial consonant clusters, for example 'bl', 'pl', 'sl', 'gr', 'tr', 'pr', and so on to extend the number of words.
- Whole words can be written on cards and children asked to first separate the cards by onset, then by rime.
- Have fun building alliterative sentences with children.
- Useful words: flow, fling, flop, flat, flag, flap, flip, flock; trip, train, trot, trod, trap, trust, travel.

Unit 7   Patterns in words

Objectives
T1 **10**   to recognise the critical features of words, for example . . . common spelling patterns;
T3 **5**   to recognise words by common spelling patterns.

Teaching focus
Introduction
This unit is designed for children to recognise that many words have spelling patterns and they are encouraged to look for them in their own work.

Using the teaching focus
The teaching focus looks at two spelling patterns. It is important that children realise these are just examples of a spelling pattern.

Class and group work
Practice   In sets of three words the spelling pattern is shown in the first word. Children are asked to find the same pattern in the following two words.
More to think about   Sets of three words are given. Each set has a different spelling pattern. Children are asked to identify the spelling pattern in each set of words.
Now try these (Copymaster 60)   Example spelling patterns are given with an example word and picture for each pattern. Children think of another word using the same spelling pattern and write the word and draw its picture.

Further ideas
- Using a familiar book, ask children to find words that are examples of the spelling patterns they have covered in this unit. Discuss and do a similar activity using other spelling patterns with which the children might be familiar.
- Provide children with more activities like those in the workbook and on the copymaster.
- Play 'hidden words' where a hidden word in a list of letters is to be found, for example a f u **g o l d** j b k. Ask children to write a spelling pattern from the word they discover.

Activity Book D

Unit	Content
8	*nd st*
9	Plurals
10	*ee oo*
11	*oa ai*
12	The word ending: *ed*
13	The word ending: *ing*
14	Vowels
	Progress Test

Unit 8 nd st

Objectives
T2 **3** to discriminate, read and spell words with final consonant clusters:
- to identify separate phonemes within words containing clusters in speech and writing;
- to blend phonemes in words with clusters for reading;
- to segment clusters into phonemes for spelling.

Teaching focus
Introduction
In a consonant cluster the two or more letter sounds that run together are pronounced, unlike a digraph that makes a single sound. This unit introduces children to the final consonant clusters 'nd' and 'st'.

Using the teaching focus
When reading the words aloud children should be encouraged to listen carefully to the constituent parts that make the 'nd' and 'st' sound.

Children writing the consonant clusters several times will help reinforce the focus of the unit. Brainstorm other 'nd' and 'st' words with the children and list them on the board.

Class and group work
Practice Children are asked to add the final consonant clusters 'nd' and 'st' to the provided word beginnings, and to write the word. Picture-cues are provided.
More to think about Words ending in the consonant clusters 'nd' and 'st' are given. Children sort the words by their endings into the table.
Now try these (Copymaster 61) Word beginnings are given. Children add the correct consonant cluster 'nd' or 'st' to make the word shown by the picture. They are asked to think of more words with 'nd' and 'st' endings.

Further ideas
- Many words end in 'st'. Write words ending in 'st' on cards. The children could arrange them into their rhyming word families, for example 'est', 'ist', 'ost' and 'ust'. Ask the children which word family is the biggest.
- A similar activity can be done for 'nd' words.
- Children can look for other examples of 'nd' and 'st' words in stories and poems.
- Children can compose their own sentences using words they have found ending in 'nd' or 'st'.
- Useful words: just, must, crust, frost, best, nest, test, vest, mist; send, bend, friend, band, sand, land.

Unit 9 Plurals

Objectives
T2 **8** to investigate and learn spellings of words with 's' for plurals.

Teaching focus
Introduction
This unit introduces changing words to plural in its simplest form – adding 's' to many nouns to make them plural.

Using the teaching focus
It is important children understand that if there is more than one of any object the word needs to be changed into its plural form.

Class and group work
Practice Using the picture-cues children add 's' to singular nouns to make them plural.
More to think about A picture represents a number of objects. The singular word is written and children have to make the plural word by adding 's'.
Now try these (Copymaster 62) Number words are given. Children fill the gaps in the sentences with one of the number words, or the singular or plural object word.

Further ideas
- Randomly, write singular and plural words which end in 's'. Ask children to separate the words into two columns, one for singular words and the other for plurals.
- Ask children to write labels for objects around the classroom, for example pens, books and so on.
- It may be appropriate while doing the above activity to discuss with the children that there are other plural endings.
- Provide children with more activities similar to those in the workbook and on the copymaster.

Unit 10 ee oo

Objectives
T3 **1** the common spelling patterns for each of the long vowel phonemes: 'ee', ('ie'),'oo':
- to identify phonemes in speech and writing;
- to blend phonemes for reading;
- to segment words into phonemes for spelling.

Teaching focus
Introduction
Both vowel sounds 'ee' and 'oo' are common and should be picked up quite quickly by children. The 'oo' vowel sound can be pronounced in three different ways though the sound covered in this unit is the most common form.

Using the teaching focus
Ask children to read the words aloud and then ask them to say the 'ee' or 'oo' sound.

To see if children can distinguish between the sounds, say either the 'ee' or 'oo' sound and ask them to write it down.

Class and group work
Practice Children encircle the letters of the long vowel phoneme 'ee' or 'oo' in words in a list. They should be encouraged to say the words aloud.

23

Activity Book D

More to think about This exercise asks children to write a word that rhymes with the key word. A picture-cue is used for each word to be found.
Now try these (Copymaster 63) Sixteen 'ee' and 'oo' words are provided. Children sort the words into the table according to the four different word families in the table – 'eed', 'eep', 'ool' and 'oot'. The children then add a further word to each column.

Further ideas
- Additional work covering 'ie' can be found on Copymaster 71.
- Each long vowel phoneme has different spelling patterns yet sounds the same, for example 'ee' in 'feet' and 'ea' in 'seat' 'oo' in 'moon, 'u-e' in 'tune', 'ew' in 'flew' and 'ue' in 'blue'. Copymasters 69 and 73 cover these long vowel phonemes.
- Ask the children to make labelled picture collages of the vowel phonemes, either individually or as a class display.
- Children could look in their reading books and find as many 'ee' and 'oo' words as they can, then sort them into groups.
- Useful words: meet, sleep, peep, seek, deep, bee, seed, deep; spoon, noon, food, room, broom, tooth, smooth.

Unit 11 oa ai

Objectives
T3 **1** the common spelling patterns for each of the long vowel phonemes: 'ai', 'oa', ('ie'):
- to identify phonemes in speech and writing;
- to blend phonemes for reading;
- to segment words into phonemes for spelling.

Teaching focus
Introduction
This unit covers the two long vowel phonemes 'oa' and 'ai'.

Using the teaching focus
Ask children to read the words aloud and then ask them to say the 'oa' and 'ai' sound.

To see if children can distinguish between the sounds, say either the 'oa' or 'ai' sound and ask them to write it down.

It is important that children focus on the sound of the spoken vowel phoneme and the visual spelling pattern.

Class and group work
Practice Children encircle the letters of the long vowel phonemes 'oa' and 'ai' in words in a list. They should be encouraged to say the words aloud.
More to think about Children are asked to fill in the missing 'oa' and 'ai' sound in words. Picture-cues are provided.
Now try these (Copymaster 64) From a box of words, the children are required to write the answer to each 'What am I?' clue.

Further ideas
- Additional work covering 'ie' can be found on Copymaster 71.
- Each long vowel phoneme has different spelling patterns yet sounds the same, for example 'ai' in 'train', 'a-e' in 'name' and 'ay' in 'play'; 'oa' in 'boat', 'o-e' in 'pole', and 'ow' in 'show'. Copymasters 70 and 72 cover these long vowel phonemes.
- Ask the children to look in stories and poems for examples of 'oa' and 'ai' words.
- Children could make labelled picture collages of the vowel phonemes, either individually or as a class display.
- Useful words: coat, stoat, cloak, croak, toast, roast, float, moan, groan; mail, jail, laid, paid, plain, main, trail.

Unit 12 ed

Objectives
T3 **6** to investigate and learn spellings of verbs with 'ed' (past tense) . . . endings.

Teaching focus
Introduction
It is important that children understand what the past is, in order to fully appreciate when to use the suffix 'ed' on the end of a verb.

Using the teaching focus
Ask the children what they did yesterday. Explain that because it has already happened it happened in the past.

Read through the teaching focus with the children and encourage them to think of their own sentences that contain the words 'jumped in'.

Class and group work
Practice Children are asked to add 'ed' to root words and then write the words.
More to think about From a selection of words children choose the words that tell them the action happened in the past. Then they have to draw a picture of two things that happened in the past.
Now try these (Copymaster 65) Choosing from 'ed' words, children fill the gap in each sentence. They then make up a sentence for each of the listed words.

Further ideas
- Link this unit with 'Text level work' for Term 3: 'Writing composition' 20, where children write simple recounts linked to personal experience (see *Framework for Teaching*, p. 25). With the children, look through their work for words ending in 'ed'.
- Look at verbs in the context of sentences.

Unit 13 ing

Objectives
T3 **6** to investigate and learn spellings of verbs with . . . 'ing' (present tense) endings.

Teaching focus
Introduction
It is important that children understand what the present is, in order to fully appreciate when to use the suffix 'ing' on the end of a verb.

Using the teaching focus
Discuss with the children what they are doing now, in the present. Make a note of their words on the board. Ask them what all the words, such as 'speaking', 'listening' or 'writing', have in common.

Read through the teaching focus with the children. Reference can be made to the 'ng' letter sound that was covered in Unit 5.

Class and group work
Practice   Children add 'ing' to verbs.
More to think about   Root words are given. Children have to add 'ing' to the root word to fill the gap in the sentence and match the picture.
Now try these (Copymaster 66)   Children answer the question 'What is Ben doing now?' by matching an 'ing' word from the boxed list to a picture and writing the word.

Further ideas
- Mime activities, for example kicking, lifting, and so on and ask children to give an 'ing' word to describe what you are doing. They can do the same thing in pairs or small groups.
- Give children 'ing' words and ask them to build them into their own sentences. Link this with 'Sentence level work' for Terms 1 and 2 (see *Framework for Teaching*, pp. 20 and 22).
- Children can look for examples of 'ing' words in stories and poems.

Class and group work
Practice   In a set of alphabet 'building blocks', children are asked to colour the five blocks that each contain a vowel.
More to think about   The vowels are given at the top of the page and children fill the missing vowel in each CVC word. Each word is picture-cued.
Now try these (Copymaster 67)   The letters of the alphabet are mixed on the page. Children write them in one of the two boxes according to whether they are vowels or consonants.

Further ideas
- The 'Now try these' copymaster can also be used to check alphabetical order if children tick the letter as they are saying it.
- Ask children to look in their reading books to find as many three-letter words as they can. They could then arrange the words according to their middle vowel. Discuss with them which vowel is used most.
- Provide children with more activities like those in the workbook and on the copymaster.

Unit 14 Vowels

Objectives
T3 **9**   the terms 'vowel' and 'consonant'.

Teaching focus
Introduction
This unit distinguishes between vowels and consonants in the alphabet. It specifically focuses on vowels.

Using the teaching focus
It is important that children say the five vowel letter sounds aloud.

Ask them to think of objects that begin with the vowel letters.

If appropriate, explain to them that all words except a few have at least one vowel in.

Introductory Book

Introductory Book

Unit	Content
1	*oo* and *u*
2	Collecting words (1)
3	*ar*
4	Adding *ing* and *ed*
5	*oi* and *oy*
6	Vowels and consonants
7	*ow* and *ou*
8	Antonyms
9	*air* and *ear*
10	Compound words
	Progress Test A
11	*or* and *aw*
12	Collecting words (2)
13	*er*, *ir* and *ur*
14	Syllables
15	Prefixes
16	*wh* and *ph*
17	Collecting words (3)
18	Suffixes
19	*ea*
20	Synonyms
	Progress Test B

Unit 1   oo and u

Objectives
T1 3   the common spelling patterns for the vowel phoneme . . . 'oo':
- to identify the phonemes in speech and writing;
- to blend the phonemes for reading;
- to segment the words into phonemes for spelling.

T1 4   to investigate and classify words with the same sounds but different spellings.

Teaching focus
Introduction
A phoneme is the smallest unit of sound in a word and 'oo' has two clearly recognised vowel phonemes. In this unit we are looking at the short 'oo' sound (for example 'good'). Visual recognition of the letter patterns that make the sounds is vital.

Using the teaching focus
Read through the teaching focus with the class, clearly stressing the vowel phonemes as the words are spoken.

Brainstorm other 'oo' and 'u' words with the children and list them on the board.

Class and group work
Practice   Words with pictures are given. Children copy the words then encircle the 'u' and underline the 'oo' words.
More to think about   A picture with labelled 'oo' and 'u' words is provided. Children sort the words according to the differently spelt phonemes into the table.
Now try these   Two words are provided for each sentence from which children choose the best word to complete the sentence. They are then required to make up three sentences that each include one of the listed 'oo' or 'u' words.

Further ideas
Word level
- Challenge children to find as many different 'oo' and 'u' words as they can.
- Make a wordsearch puzzle, or ask children to do so, including as many 'oo' and 'u' words as you can.
- Play the alphabet game – each group of children needs a set of cards with each letter of the alphabet on. A word with 'oo' or 'u' is said and the children have to lay down the word spelt correctly, as quickly as possible. If the word has any double letters, paper and pencils must be provided for writing a card for the missing letter.
- If appropriate, this work can be linked with Unit 18 on the suffix 'ful'.
- Useful words: good, book, look, hood, wood, cook, took, brook, shook, crook; pull, bull, put, bully, fully, useful, helpful, hopeful, thoughtful, painful, spiteful, careful.

Sentence level
- Give children more 'oo' and 'u' words to include in sentences of their own. Ensure the sentences begin with a capital letter and end with a full stop.

Text level
- Read to children from a text that includes the vowel phoneme, asking the children to identify the 'oo' and 'u' sounds.
- Write fun rhymes using 'oo' and 'u' words.

Unit 2   Collecting words (1)

Objectives
T1 10   new words from reading linked to particular topics, to build individual collections of personal interest or significant words.

Teaching focus
Introduction
Many KS1 word books and dictionaries contain lists of words, not only organised alphabetically, but also organised thematically according to topic. If possible begin by having a look at some of these.

Discuss why it might be helpful to collect words and have them organised in this way (for example, where spellings can be easily found for checking and to give ideas when writing).

Name a few topics (like the weather and shopping) and ask for suggestions of the sorts of words that might be listed.

Using the teaching focus
Look at the labelled diagram, and read the words, with the class.

Discuss what other words could have been included and write these on the board.

Discuss how the lines linking each label to the picture are helpful. Ask the children what problems there might be if the lines were not there.

Class and group work
Practice   Children are asked to complete missing words from sentences, using the words from the labelled picture above.

Introductory Book

More to think about The names of parts of the body are hidden in mini wordsearch puzzles. Children are asked to find and write these down.
Now try these An outline picture of a child's body is given, with various parts of the body labelled with a number. Children are asked to write the correct name of each part of the body corresponding to each number.

Further ideas
Word level
- List the names of the parts of the body covered in the exercises. Underline any long vowel phonemes, for example 'ose' in 'nose', and vowel phonemes, for example 'ou' in 'mouth', or any other significant spelling points, for example silent 'w' in 'wrist'.
- Ask children to think of another word containing these letter patterns, or another word that rhymes.
- Use the words for practice in using the Look Say Cover Write Check method for learning words.
- Consider how many of these words can have an 's' added to the end of them.
- Encourage children to collect lists of words related to topics being covered in other subjects in the classroom.

Sentence level
Ask the children to draw around their hands and label the parts of the hand (for example, palm, fingers, thumb, fingernails, knuckles, wrist) using labels and arrows.

Text level
Ask the children to write a description of a friend, using some of the vocabulary they have learnt.

Unit 3   ar

Objectives
T1 3   the common spelling patterns for the vowel phoneme . . . 'ar':
- to identify the phonemes in speech and writing;
- to blend the phonemes for reading;
- to segment the words into phonemes for spelling.

Teaching focus
Introduction
A phoneme is the smallest unit of sound in a word. Visual recognition of the letter pattern that makes the sound is vital.

Using the teaching focus
Read through the teaching focus with the children, clearly stressing the vowel phoneme as the words are said.

Brainstorm other 'ar' words with children and list them on the board.

Class and group work
Practice Pictures of 'ar' words are given. Children are asked to add 'ar' to complete words, then to write the word that matches the picture.
More to think about Children sort the 'ar' words provided into a table of 'ar' and 'art' rhyming word families.
Now try these Two words are provided for each sentence from which children choose the best word to complete the sentence. They are then required to make up three sentences that each include one of the three listed 'ar' words.

Further ideas
Word level
- Put children in teams to find as many 'ar' words as possible. Make a game of this by giving a time limit. Ask the children to check the words in a dictionary.
- Give children different 'ar' words and ask them to sort them according to the word endings, for example 'ark', 'art', 'ard', 'arm', 'arn', and so on.
- Play the alphabet game. Each group of children needs a set of cards with each letter of the alphabet on. A word with 'ar' is said and the children have to lay down the word spelt correctly, as quickly as possible. If the word has any double letters, paper and pencils should be provided for writing a card for the missing letter.
- If appropriate, this work can be linked with Unit 4 on the suffixes 'ing' and 'ed'.
- Useful words: arm, darn, barge, car, harm, harp, hard, spark, large, charge, scarf, march, charm, farm, sharp.

Sentence level
- Give children more 'ar' words to include in sentences of their own. Ensure the sentences begin with a capital letter and end with a full stop.

Text level
- Using a piece of text, ask children to look through it picking out the words with the 'ar' phoneme.

Unit 4   Adding ing and ed

Objectives
T1 7   to use word endings, for example 's' (plural), 'ed' (past tense), 'ing' (present tense) to support their reading and spelling.

Teaching focus
Introduction
Children need to have an appreciation of the past and present in order to understand when the suffixes 'ing' or 'ed' are used in this context.

Using the teaching focus
Ask children what they did yesterday, explain that because it has already happened it is in the past. Discuss with them what they are doing now, in the present. Make a note of the words on the board. Ask them what their words (for example 'speaking', 'listening' or 'writing') have in common.

Work through the example in the teaching focus.

Ask children to suggest two sentences that reflect the changing tense of the word 'jump' and other similar examples.

Class and group work
Practice Words ending in 'ing' and 'ed' are provided. The children are asked to copy them and circle the 'ing' and underline the 'ed' endings.
More to think about A table with three columns, one containing a list of words, the second headed '+ ing', and the third headed '+ ed' is to be completed.
Now try these Two words are provided for each sentence from which children choose the best word to complete the sentence. They are then required to make up three sentences that each include one of the three listed 'ing' and 'ed' words.

Introductory Book

Further ideas
Word level
- The word ending 's' (plural) is covered separately on Copymaster 74.
- Ask the children to write five actions that happened in school yesterday (in the past), for example 'worked' or 'played', and then a further five things that are happening now, for example 'talking' or 'counting'.

Sentence level
- Write some sentences that have either 'ing' or 'ed' words in the wrong context. Ask the children to read them, identifying and correcting each wrong word, for example 'Dad snoring loudly last night!'

Text level
- Read to the children from a text that includes 'ing' or 'ed' endings, asking them to identify those words. They can do this by either raising their hands or quietly keeping a tally and discussing the number of 'ing' or 'ed' words they found.

Unit 5   oi and oy

Objectives
T1 **3**   the common spelling patterns for the vowel phoneme . . . 'oy':
- to identify the phonemes in speech and writing;
- to blend the phonemes for reading;
- to segment the words into phonemes for spelling.

T1 **4**   to investigate and classify words with the same sounds but different spellings.

Teaching focus
Introduction
A phoneme is the smallest unit of sound in a word. The vowel sound/letter pattern 'oi' never appears at the end of a word. Visual recognition of the letter pattern that makes the sound is vital.

Using the teaching focus
Read the teaching focus with the children, stressing the vowel phonemes as the words are said.

Brainstorm other 'oi' and 'oy' words with the children and list them on the board.

Class and group work
Practice   Children are required to write the word, from those provided, that matches the picture.
More to think about   Children complete the sentences with an appropriate 'oi' and 'oy' word from those provided.
Now try these   Words are to be sorted into a table with a column for 'oi' and one for 'oy' words. Children choose three of the words and make up three sentences, each to include one of the words.

Further ideas
Word level
- Make a wordsearch puzzle, or ask children to do so, including as many 'oi' and 'oy' words as possible.
- Use some 'oi' and 'oy' words for practice in using the Look Say Cover Write Check method for learning words.
- Useful words: oil, boil, soil, spoil, coin, join, joint, point, choice, voice; boy, joy, toy, enjoy, employ.

Sentence level
- Give children more 'oi' and 'oy' words to include in correctly punctuated sentences of their own.
- Provide children with additional work practising the activity in the 'More to think about' section.

Text level
- Draw a picture of a boy holding a coin, pointing at some spilt oil on a toy, and so on. Ask children to label the 'oi' and 'oy' words.

Unit 6   Vowels and consonants

Objectives
T1 **8**   to secure understanding and use of the terms 'vowel' and 'consonant'.

Teaching focus
Introduction
This unit distinguishes between vowels and consonants in the alphabet. It reinforces the role vowels play in words.

Using the teaching focus
Ask children to read the alphabet aloud, focusing on the names of the letters.

Pick out the vowels with them, reinforcing the sound the letter makes.

Read through the teaching focus together, then ask them questions about what they have learnt, for example 'How many vowels are there?', 'What sound does "a" make?'

Class and group work
Practice   This requires that children recognise the vowel in CVC words. They underline the vowel in each picture-cued word.
More to think about   A picture with part-labelled items requires the children to fill in the missing vowel to complete the labels.
Now try these   Words are to be sorted into a table according to the vowel found in them. Then children need to find a further two words to add to each column.

Further ideas
Word level
- Using some of the high frequency words on Copymaster 78, ask children to write the words out and underline the vowels in them.
- Give children a list of high frequency words and a vowel. Ask them to write down all the words with that vowel in and then to read the words back to you.

Sentence level
- Write out some simple sentences with the vowels missing. Ask the children to fill in the missing letters so the sentence makes sense, for example 'Th_ c_t s_t _n th_ m_t' becomes 'The cat sat on the mat'.

Text level
- Ask the children to look in their reading books and find as many three-letter words as they can. Ask them to keep a tally of which vowel occurs most often. Simple block graphs to show their results can make an effective display.

Introductory Book

Unit 7 ow and ou

Objectives
T1 **3** the common spelling patterns for the vowel phoneme . . . 'ow':
- to identify the phonemes in speech and writing;
- to blend the phonemes for reading;
- to segment the words into phonemes for spelling.

T1 **4** to investigate and classify words with the same sounds but different spellings.

Teaching focus
Introduction
A phoneme is the smallest unit of sound in a word. Visual recognition of the letter patterns that make the sounds is vital.

Using the teaching focus
Read through the teaching focus with the class, stressing the vowel phonemes as the words are spoken.

Brainstorm other 'ow' and 'ou' words with the children and list them on the board.

Class and group work
Practice Children are required to copy the number of the picture and write the word, from the four provided, that matches the picture.

More to think about Children choose the most suitable word, from the 'ow' and 'ou' words provided, to complete each sentence.

Now try these Words are to be sorted into a table with a column for 'ow' words and one for 'ou' words. The children choose three of the words and make up three sentences, each to include one of the words.

Further ideas
Word level
- Play the alphabet game. Each group of children needs a set of cards with each letter of the alphabet on. A word with 'ow' or 'ou' is said and the children have to lay down the word spelt correctly, as quickly as possible. If the word has any double letters paper and pencils should be provided for writing a card for the missing letter.
- Useful words: cow, how, now, howl, growl, prowl, down, town, gown, brown, crowd; our, out, about, scout, shout, trout, loud, cloud, mouse, mouth, count, south.

Sentence level
- Give children more 'ow' or 'ou' words to include in correctly punctuated sentences of their own.

Text level
- Ask children to write a description of a dog using as many 'ow' and 'ou' words as they can.

Unit 8 Antonyms

Objectives
T2 **11** the use of antonyms: collect, discuss differences of meaning and spelling.

Teaching focus
Introduction
Antonyms are words with opposite meanings, for example 'hot', 'cold'. Sometimes a word may have more than one word as an antonym, for example 'big': 'small', 'tiny', 'little', 'titchy'.

Introduce the idea of opposites by reminding children of the nursery rhyme 'Jack Sprat would eat no fat, his wife would eat no lean, and so between them both, you see, they licked the platter clean': they were as different as possible from each other.

Using the teaching focus
Look at the picture and the words with the class. Read the definition of an antonym.

Brainstorm other antonyms which have opposite meanings.

Ask children to suggest pairs of antonyms.

If this proves a little difficult, provide children with one word and ask for its opposite, for example 'empty', 'near', 'left', 'run', 'slow'.

Class and group work
Practice Two lists of words are provided. Children are asked to match each word in the left-hand column with an antonym in the right-hand column.

More to think about Children are given six words. Their opposites are hidden in mini wordsearch puzzles for them to find.

Now try these Sentences are provided with gaps. Children have to supply suitable antonyms for each gap after reading and predicting the missing antonym by using grammatical and context cues.

Further ideas
Word level
- Play the antonym game. Provide a wide range of word cards of adjectives and verbs that have possible antonyms. In pairs, children have to take a card and suggest a suitable antonym. An extension of this is to write down the antonyms, spelling them correctly.
- Children could play antonym pairs with word cards, using the same principle as Pelmanism.
- Provide children with sentence completion activities based on the pattern 'An apple is sweet but a lemon is . . .'

Sentence level
- Explain that Annie Antonym always changes sentences into the opposite meaning! Ask children to rewrite sentences and change the underlined word, for example, 'The children were very good'.

Text level
- Look for other nursery rhymes and poems containing opposites.

Unit 9 air and ear

Objectives
T2 **2** the common spelling patterns for the vowel phoneme . . . 'air':
- to identify the phonemes in speech and writing;
- to blend the phonemes for reading;
- to segment the words into phonemes for spelling.

T1 **4** to investigate and classify words with the same sounds but different spellings.

29

Introductory Book

Teaching focus
Introduction
These vowel phonemes, 'air' and 'ear', have been grouped together but often they are taught separately. They can be difficult for children to recognise, particularly because both 'air' and 'ear' are words themselves with different pronunciations. Children need these differences illustrated and discussed.

Using the teaching focus
Work through the teaching focus, encouraging children to participate verbally. Visual recognition of the letter patterns that make the sounds is vital.

Class and group work
Practice Children underline the same sound as 'air' in words which are picture-cued.
More to think about Six labelled pictures with 'air' and 'ear' words are provided. The words need sorting into the table of word families.
Now try these Two words are provided in each sentence for the children to choose the most appropriate word to complete the sentence. They are then required to make up three sentences that each include one of the three listed 'air' or 'ear' words.

Further ideas
Word level
- The vowel phonemes 'are' and 'ere' are covered separately on Copymaster 75.
- When you feel the children can recognise that 'air', 'are', 'ere' and 'ear' make similar sounds then activities where all four are used together can be introduced. Provide additional work for practising the activities in the unit.
- Useful words: pear, tear, wear, swear; air, fair, hair, chair, pair, flair, stair; there, where; scare, bare, fare, care, rare, hare, mare, share.

Sentence level
- Ask children to write sentences beginning with the personal pronoun 'I' using 'air', 'are', 'ere' and 'ear' words.

Text level
- The children could study in detail a section of text and do a tally of the letter patterns of the phonemes being studied that are used most and least often.

Unit 10   Compound words

Objectives
T2 4   to split familiar oral and written compound words into their component parts.

Teaching focus
Introduction
Children often enjoy working on compound words, especially when they discover how many compound words there are.

Using the teaching focus
Read through the teaching focus with the children, stressing the fact that the smaller words can stand completely independently as words themselves.

Class and group work
Practice Children are asked to make the compound word, which is picture-cued, from two small words.
More to think about Children are given the compound word and are asked to write the two short words it is made from.
Now try these Children are given two pictures that represent individual words. They have to work out what the pictures represent and then add the two words together to make the compound word. Each compound word then needs to be written into a sentence.

Further ideas
Word level
- Allow children to experiment in creating their own compound words. They could draw pictures to illustrate them. This can make an effective class display.
- Groups of children can be given different root words (see below), they then have to think of as many different compound words as possible. The words can be hung from the root word to make a mobile.
- Useful root words: snow, foot, sun, every, ear, rain, some, wind.

Sentence level
- Ask children to write correctly punctuated sentences using two or three compound words with the same root word, for example 'The snowball hit the snowman and knocked his hat off!'

Text level
- Children can be challenged to see how many compound words they can think of themselves or how many compound words they can find in a piece of text.

Unit 11   or and aw

Objectives
T2 2   the common spelling patterns for the vowel phoneme . . . 'or':
- to identify the phonemes in speech and writing;
- to blend the phonemes for reading;
- to segment the words into phonemes for spelling.

T1 4   to investigate and classify words with the same sounds but different spellings.

Teaching focus
Introduction
Although these phonemes can make the same sound, in many dialects throughout the United Kingdom they do not. It is very important that allowances for this are made when working through this unit.

Using the teaching focus
Work through the teaching focus, encouraging children to participate verbally. Visual recognition of the letter patterns that make the sounds is vital.

Class and group work
Practice Children underline the same sound as 'or' in words which are picture-cued.
More to think about Labelled pictures with 'aw' and 'or' words are provided. The words are to be sorted into a table of 'aw' and 'or' word families.
Now try these Two words are provided in each sentence

Introductory Book

for children to choose the most appropriate word to complete the sentence. They are then required to make up three sentences that each include one of the three listed 'aw' and 'or' words.

Further ideas
Word level
- The vowel phonemes 'au' and 'ore' are covered separately on Copymaster 76.
- When you feel the children can recognise that 'or', 'aw', 'au' and 'ore' make similar sounds then activities where all four are used together can be introduced. Provide additional work for practising the activities found in the unit.
- Make a wordsearch puzzle, or ask the children to do so, including as many 'or' and 'aw' words as possible.
- Useful words: horse, horn, cord, fork, lord, scorn, snort, born, worn; core, store, shore, score, tore, more; law, paw, saw, thaw, draw, lawn, dawn, drawn, crawl, hawk; caught, taught, sauce, August, author, because, haunt, pause, autograph.

Sentence level
- Ask children to write sentences beginning with the personal pronoun 'I' using 'or' and 'aw' words.

Text level
- After doing a word hunt in a piece of text children could do some activities focusing on rhyming words.

Unit 12   Collecting words (2)

Objectives
T2 **10**   new words from reading linked to particular topics, to build individual collections of personal interest or significant words.

Teaching focus
Introduction

Many KS1 word books and dictionaries contain lists of words, not only organised alphabetically, but also organised thematically according to topic. If possible begin by having a look at some of these.

Discuss why it might be helpful to collect words and have them organised in this way (for example, where spellings can be easily found for checking and to give ideas when writing).

Name a few topics (like the weather and shopping) and ask for suggestions of the sorts of words that might be listed.

Using the teaching focus

Look at the picture and labels with the class. Read the labels together. Discuss what the words have in common. Ask what sort of story they relate to.

Ask the children to suggest other useful words that might come in handy when writing traditional or fairy stories. List these on the board.

Class and group work
Practice   Children are asked to match up sentence beginnings and endings containing some of the words from the picture in the teaching focus section.
More to think about   In this activity children are required to write the phrase, based on a fairy story theme, from those provided, that matches the picture.

Now try these   A list of nouns related to fairy stories is supplied. The task is to classify these under three headings – 'people', 'animals' and 'places'.

Further ideas
Word level
- Use some of the words covered in the unit to stimulate spelling activities, for example, talk about tricky bits of words; group words according to spelling patterns; look for small words within longer words; think of related rhyming words, and so on.
- Try to think of additional story words under the 'people', 'animals' and 'places' headings in the 'Now try these' section.
- Encourage children to collect lists of words related to topics being covered in other subjects in the classroom.

Sentence level
- Practise using commas to separate items in lists, using thematic word lists.

Text level
- Relate 'book' words to books being read, when discussing author, publisher, covers, titles, chapters and so on.

Unit 13   er, ir and ur

Objectives
T2 **2**   the common spelling patterns for the vowel phoneme . . .'er':
- to identify the phonemes in speech and writing;
- to blend the phonemes for reading;
- to segment the words into phonemes for spelling.

T1 **4**   to investigate and classify words with the same sounds but different spellings.

Teaching focus
Introduction

Although these phonemes can make the same sound, in many dialects throughout the United Kingdom they do not. It is very important that allowances for this are made when working through this unit.

Using the teaching focus

Work through the teaching focus, encouraging children to participate verbally. Visual recognition of the letter patterns that make the sounds is vital.

Class and group work
Practice   This requires the children to underline the same sound as 'ir' in 'bird' in words which are picture-cued.
More to think about   Nine labelled pictures with 'ir', 'er' and 'ur' words are provided. Children sort the words into the table of 'ir', 'er' and 'ur' word families.
Now try these   Two words are provided in each sentence for the children to choose the most appropriate word to complete the sentence. They are then required to make up three sentences that each include one of the listed 'ir', 'er' and 'ur' words.

Further ideas
Word level
- Play the alphabet game. Each group of children needs a set of cards with each letter of the alphabet on. A word with 'er', 'ir' or 'ur' is said and the children have to lay down the word spelt correctly, as quickly

31

Introductory Book

as possible. If the word has any double letters, paper and pencils should be provided for writing a card for the missing letter.
- Useful words: her, herd, term, nerve, perch, letter, teacher, butter, litter; stir, bird, third, shirt, shirt, swirl, first, chirp, birth; burn, turn, curl, surf, purse, nurse, burst, burnt, hurt, church.

Sentence level
- Give children more 'er', 'ir' and 'ur' words to include in correctly punctuated sentences of their own.

Text level
- Children can collect as many 'er', 'ir' or 'ur' words as possible and then check their words in a dictionary. They could draw a simple block graph illustrating the frequency of the words.
- Children could draw and label a picture with as many words that use the 'er', 'ir' or 'ur' phoneme as they can.

Unit 14   Syllables

Objectives
T2 5   to discriminate, orally, syllables in multi-syllabic words using children's names and words from their reading. Extend to written forms and note syllable boundary in speech and writing.

Teaching focus
Introduction
Children enjoy working on syllables. It provides them with a new way of breaking up words that ultimately can aid their spelling.

Using the teaching focus
Encourage children to say the words slowly, clapping the beats as they do. Any number of words can be used as an example of syllables until they get the idea. Point out that some words have only one syllable. Another way of stressing syllables in words is to ask children to speak like robots (pinching their noses!).

Class and group work
Practice   Words are broken down into all but their last syllable which is left for children to fill in.
More to think about   Children are asked to break down five words into their syllables.
Now try these   First, children have to count how many syllables there are in six words, then they have to copy a table and write two one-, two- and three-syllable words in each column.

Further ideas
Word level
- Write a selection of words with various numbers of syllables on cards and ask the children to sort them by number of syllables.
- Do syllable-counting activities using the children's names; for example, sort the children by the number of syllables in their name.

Sentence level
- When recording syllable activities with the children's names, check the use of capitals.

Text level
- Beat out syllables while reading favourite poems aloud.

Unit 15   Prefixes

Objectives
T2 8   to spell words with common prefixes, for example 'un', 'dis', to indicate the negative.

Teaching focus
Introduction
A prefix is a morpheme – a small unit of meaning – that is added to the beginning of a word. When added to a word it changes the meaning of the word. The spelling of the root word always stays the same when adding a prefix.

Using the teaching focus
Children need to appreciate what a prefix is. They need to become familiar with the letter patterns of 'un' and 'dis'. Look at the words 'tie' and 'appear' with the class, then add the prefix to the words and show how the meaning of the words changes.

Class and group work
Practice   Children are asked to recognise and underline the prefix in four words.
More to think about   Three 'un' and three 'dis' prefixes are to be added to different root words.
Now try these   Four sentences are given. Children choose one of the four given words to fill the gap in each sentence, and are asked to find more words with the prefixes 'un' and 'dis'.

Further ideas
Word level
- Challenge children to find as many different 'un' and 'dis' prefixed words as they can, using a dictionary to help.
- Make a wordsearch puzzle, or ask the children to do so, including as many 'un' and 'dis' words as possible.
- Useful words: untie, unlock, unlucky, unequal, unborn, unlike, unhappy; dislike, disobey, disagree, distaste, distrust, disagree.

Sentence level
- Write out some simple sentences with words that have the prefixes missing. Children fill in the missing letters so the sentence makes sense.
- Give the children more 'un' and 'dis' prefixed words to include in correctly punctuated sentences of their own.

Text level
- Look for words that have been prefixed with 'un' and 'dis' in a text. Check that the child understands the meaning of the words.

Unit 16   wh and ph

Objectives
T2 3   to read and spell words containing the digraph 'wh', 'ph', ('ch').

Teaching focus
Introduction
A digraph is two letters representing one sound. Many of the question words begin with 'wh', for example 'when', 'where', 'what' and so on. There are a large number of 'ph' words but many may be too advanced for the spelling of this age range, for example 'physical', 'graphic', 'pheasant'.

Introductory Book

Using the teaching focus
Work through the teaching focus with the children, encouraging them to participate verbally. Visual recognition of the letter patterns that make the sounds is vital.

Class and group work
Practice Children are required to underline the 'wh' or 'ph' digraphs in picture-cued words.
More to think about Six 'What do you think I am?' sentences and six words that include 'wh' or 'ph' in their spelling are provided. Children answer the puzzle with the correct word from the six given.
Now try these First, the children are asked to refer back through the unit noting all the 'wh' and 'ph' words and recording them in the table. Then they are asked to add a further three words in each column, using a dictionary to help.

Further ideas
Word level
- The digraph 'ch' as in 'chemist' is covered separately on Copymaster 77.
- Ask children to find as many 'wh', 'ph' or 'ch' words as possible by using dictionaries. Make it into a game by giving a time limit.
- Useful words: when, where, what, who, why, wheel, wheat, whip, white; photograph, dolphin, pheasant, telephone, physical, alphabet, elephant, sphere; Christmas, school, chemist, stomach, ache, echo, choir, anchor.

Sentence level
- Give the children 'wh', 'ph' and 'ch' words to include in correctly punctuated sentences of their own.
- Give children statements and ask them to turn them into questions using 'wh' words and add question marks.

Text level
- Ask children to plan an interview with someone, for example a caretaker, a headteacher, a grandmother or a shop owner, and write questions beginning with 'wh' words.

Unit 17 Collecting words (3)

Objectives
T3 9 new words from reading linked to particular topics, to build individual collections of personal interest or significant words.

Teaching focus
Introduction
Many KS1 word books and dictionaries contain lists of words, not only organised alphabetically, but also organised thematically according to topic. If possible begin by having a look at some of these.

Discuss why it might be helpful to collect words and have them organised in this way (for example, to refer to for spellings and to give ideas when writing).

Name a few topics (like the weather and shopping) and ask for suggestions of the sorts of words that might be listed.

Using the teaching focus
Look at the picture, read and discuss the labelled words with the class. Talk about the topic of transport and what other words could have been included. List these on the board, discussing their spellings in the process.

Class and group work
Practice This is a sentence completion activity. By using the context of each sentence the children have to choose the most appropriate word from the two given for each sentence.
More to think about Children are supplied with words that are types of transport. Their task is to classify these under three headings, depending on whether each is a land, sea or air mode of transport.
Now try these In this activity children are given various vehicles and have to arrange them in alphabetical order according to their first letter.

Further ideas
Word level
- Brainstorm as many types of transport as possible. Children should think of different ways of classifying and categorising the types, for example by number of wheels, by means of propulsion, whether it is air, land or sea-related, and so on.
- Some of the words can be used as a basis for spelling activities.
- Children could organise the words into alphabetical order.
- A simple dictionary should be used to look up the definitions of different types of transport.
- Encourage children to collect lists of words related to topics being covered in other subjects in the classroom.

Sentence level
- Ask children to turn a set of given statements about different types of transport into questions, practising using 'wh' words to open each question.

Text level
- Children can practise using contents pages and indexes of books about transport to find information on their theme.

Unit 18 Suffixes

Objectives
T3 7 To spell words with common suffixes, for example 'ful', 'ly'.

Teaching focus
Introduction
A suffix is a morpheme – a small unit of meaning – that is added to the end of a word. When added to a word it changes the meaning of the word.

Using the teaching focus
First, children need to appreciate what a suffix is. They need to become familiar with the letter patterns of 'ful' and 'ly'. Look at the words 'help' and 'quick' then add the suffix to the words and show how the meaning of the words changes.

Class and group work
Practice Five words are given. Children are asked to add the suffixes 'ful' and 'ly' to the words.
More to think about Six words ending in 'ful' or 'ly' are to be sorted into the table.

33

Introductory Book

Now try these Four words are provided for the children to choose the most appropriate word to complete each sentence. They then make up three sentences that each include one of the listed 'ful' or 'ly' words.

Further ideas

Word level
- Challenge the children to find the most words with the 'ful' or 'ly' suffixes, even allowing time at home to extend the challenge.
- Make a wordsearch puzzle, or ask the children to do so, including as many 'ful' or 'ly' words as possible.
- Useful words: careful, thankful, painful, wonderful, helpful, useful, shameful; smartly, lovely, nicely, safely, lately, likely, wisely.

Sentence level
- Write out some simple sentences with words with the suffixes missing. Ask children to fill in the missing letters so the sentence makes sense.
- Give children more words with suffixes to include in correctly punctuated sentences of their own.

Text level
- Find examples of the suffixes 'ful' or 'ly' in words in a text. Check the children understand each word and how it is used.

Unit 19 ea

Objectives
T3 3 discriminate, spell and read the phonemes 'ear' ('hear') and 'ea' ('head').
T3 6 to investigate words which have the same spelling patterns but different sounds.

Teaching focus

Introduction
Children need to concentrate hard on the 'ea' sounds they hear in words in order to distinguish between them. Visual recognition of the letter patterns that make the sounds is vital.

Using the teaching focus
Read through the teaching focus with the children, highlighting the phonemes as they say the words.

Brainstorm and list other 'ea' words with the children.

Class and group work

Practice Children are asked to distinguish between different 'ea' sounds by placing words into two columns.
More to think about This exercise asks children to choose a word from the six provided that rhymes with the picture-cued key word.
Now try these Children are provided with a clue, for each of five words, to work out the missing letters of the word that contains the 'ea' sound.

Further ideas

Word level
- A big head could be drawn and used as a class display. On one side of the head children can add 'ear' words and on the other 'ea' words.
- Useful words: ear, hear, gear, near, tear, year, clear, smear, beard; dead, head, spread, instead, thread.

Sentence level
- Write out sentences with 'ear' and 'ea' words. Transpose some words so the children have to reorder the words so the sentence makes sense; for example, 'This the year is very weather hot' becomes 'This year the weather is very hot'.

Text level
- Children could write humorous silly sentences, rhymes, tongue twisters and phrases using 'ea' words.

Unit 20 Synonyms

Objectives
T3 10 to use synonyms and other alternative words/phrases that express the same or similar meanings; to collect, discuss similarities and shades of meaning and use to extend and enhance writing.

Teaching focus

Introduction
Synonyms may be defined as words which have the same, or very similar, meaning, such as 'wet' and 'damp'. They may be used to avoid the over-use of any words, for example 'got', 'said', 'nice', 'good', and so on. Synonyms are also useful because they add variety.

Use the weather to introduce the idea. Talk about the kind of day it is, for example dull and dreary, overcast; damp and drizzly, and so on.

Using the teaching focus
Look at the picture with the children, and read the caption.

Draw attention to the adjectives in bold. Point out that they are very similar in meaning. Use the word 'synonym' in your explanation.

Ask the children to supply other related synonyms such as 'joyful' or 'pleased'.

Class and group work

Practice Children are supplied with six adjectives and asked to pair them off with six synonyms.
More to think about Six sets of four words are given, each of which contains a pair of synonyms. The children have to identify the pairs of words.
Now try these Children are given five sentences, each with an accompanying sentence. The accompanying sentences are incomplete. Children have to complete each with one of the five given words so that it has a similar meaning to the first sentence.

Further ideas

Word level
- Provide children with a list of adjectives and ask them to supply a synonym for each.
- Give children some odd word out exercises in which two of the three words are synonyms.
- Introduce children to a very simple thesaurus and discuss its function, showing them how it works.

Sentence level
- Encourage the children to construct some sentences of their own, correctly punctuated, using some of the pairs of synonyms from the exercises.

Text level
- Look for examples of synonyms in stories and texts being read in class.

High frequency words (Years 1/2)

Objectives
To read on sight the high frequency words to be taught by the end of Year 2.

Copymaster 78: Year 1/2 High frequency words checklist, and Copymaster 89: Additional high frequency words
These may be used for a variety of purposes.
1. They may be given to children:
   - to be stuck onto card. The words may be cut out and used as flash words for learning on sight or for making sentences or phrases with;
   - to be stuck onto card. The words may be cut out and used in a variety of games, for example snap, Pelmanism, the high frequency words game (see below), or the fishing game. To make the fishing game, put a paper clip on each word card and make a simple rod and line with a magnet on the end. Put the 'fish' into a box. Let the children fish the words out one at a time and keep each word they know. They see how many 'fish' they can catch;
   - to be used as record sheets by each child to colour in as words are learnt and remembered.
2. They may be used by the teacher:
   - as a prompt or test card to show children to check which words they know;
   - as an individual record sheet for each child;
   - to be pasted on card and used as the caller's cards in word lotto games, and as the caller's check-up card to keep a note of which words have been called during the course of a game.

Copymasters 79–82 and 90: High frequency words lotto cards
These may be stuck onto card, cut out and used as lotto cards by children. There are 12 separate cards covering the high frequency words and a further three cards covering additional words, encouraging word recognition.

Copymaster 83: High frequency words game
This is a game for two to four children who need a dice and a counter each and a set of high frequency word cards placed face down on the desk. Children take turns to throw the dice. They must turn over the card from the top of the pile and read the high frequency word before they can move their counter the number shown on the dice. If they cannot read the word, they cannot move their counter. The high frequency word is put on one side and the next child throws the dice and repeats the above. The winner is the first child to reach the end of the course. This game encourages word recognition.

Copymasters 84–85: Writing high frequency words
These copymasters encourage children to look carefully at a selection of high frequency words, noticing especially their shape, length and spelling.

Copymasters 86–88: Using high frequency words
Copymaster 86: provides an open-ended activity encouraging children to compose sentences involving the use of a selection of high frequency words. The subject of the writing can either be teacher-led or the choice of the child.

Copymasters 87 and 88: have picked on specific high frequency words that have the same sounds but different spellings. The word definitions have been left for the teacher to discuss with the children. However, the following are possible definitions:
'**to**' is used when a point or place is being shown;
'**too**' is used instead of the word 'also';
'**two**' is used to write the number two;
'**there**' is usually used when you write about a place;
'**their**' is usually used when you write about something belonging to someone.

Copymasters 91–92: Additional words
These copymasters give children specific practice on the additional words.

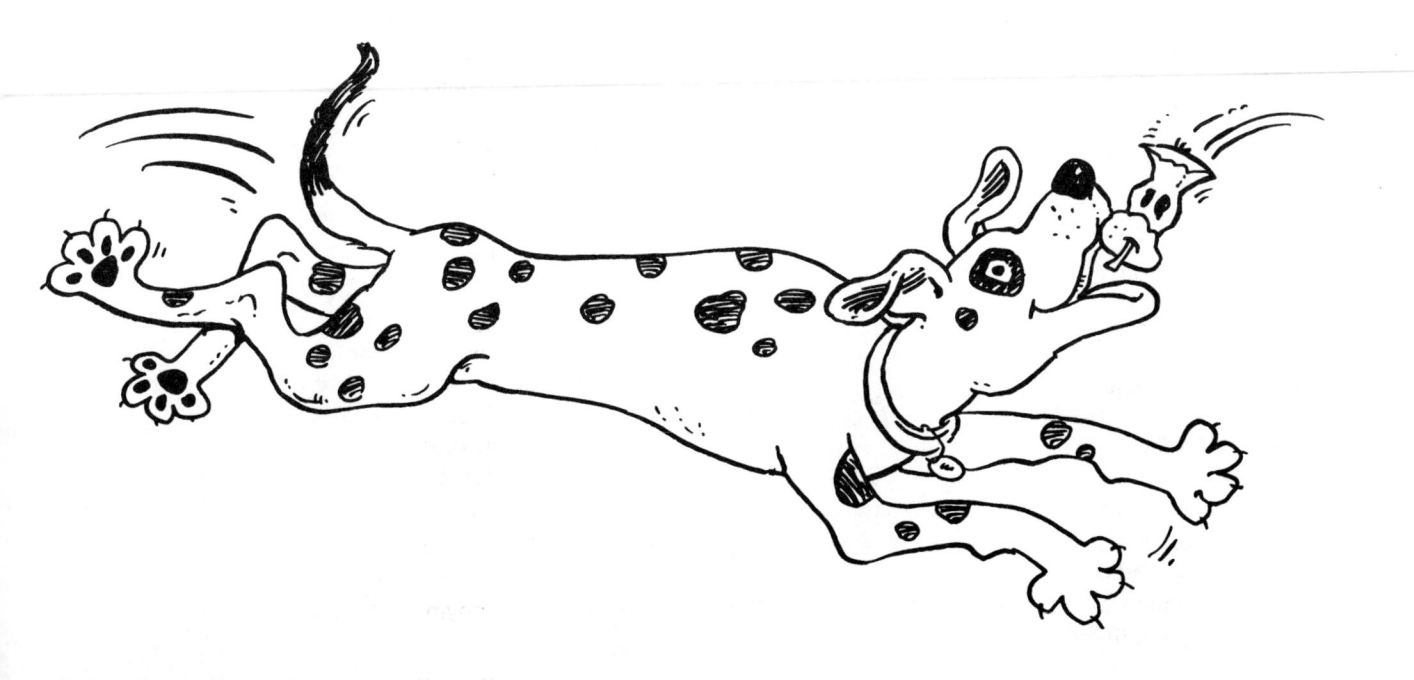

Copymasters

Year R: Initial letter sounds 1–26

Year R: 'Now try these' extension activities 27–40

Year R: Extra 41

Year R: High frequency words 42–53

Year 1: 'Now try these' extension activities 54–67

Year 1: Extras 68–73

Year 2: Extras 74–77

Years 1/2: High frequency words 78–92

Name _____

COPYMASTER 1

Colour the pictures that begin with a.

a

Circle the letter a.

a	b	c	d	e	f	g
h	i	j	k	l	m
n	o	p	q	r	s	t
u	v	w	x	y	z

Write the letter a.

Focus on Word Work © Louis Fidge and Sarah Lindsay, HarperCollins*Publishers* 1998

COPYMASTER 2

Name _____

Colour the pictures that begin with **b**.

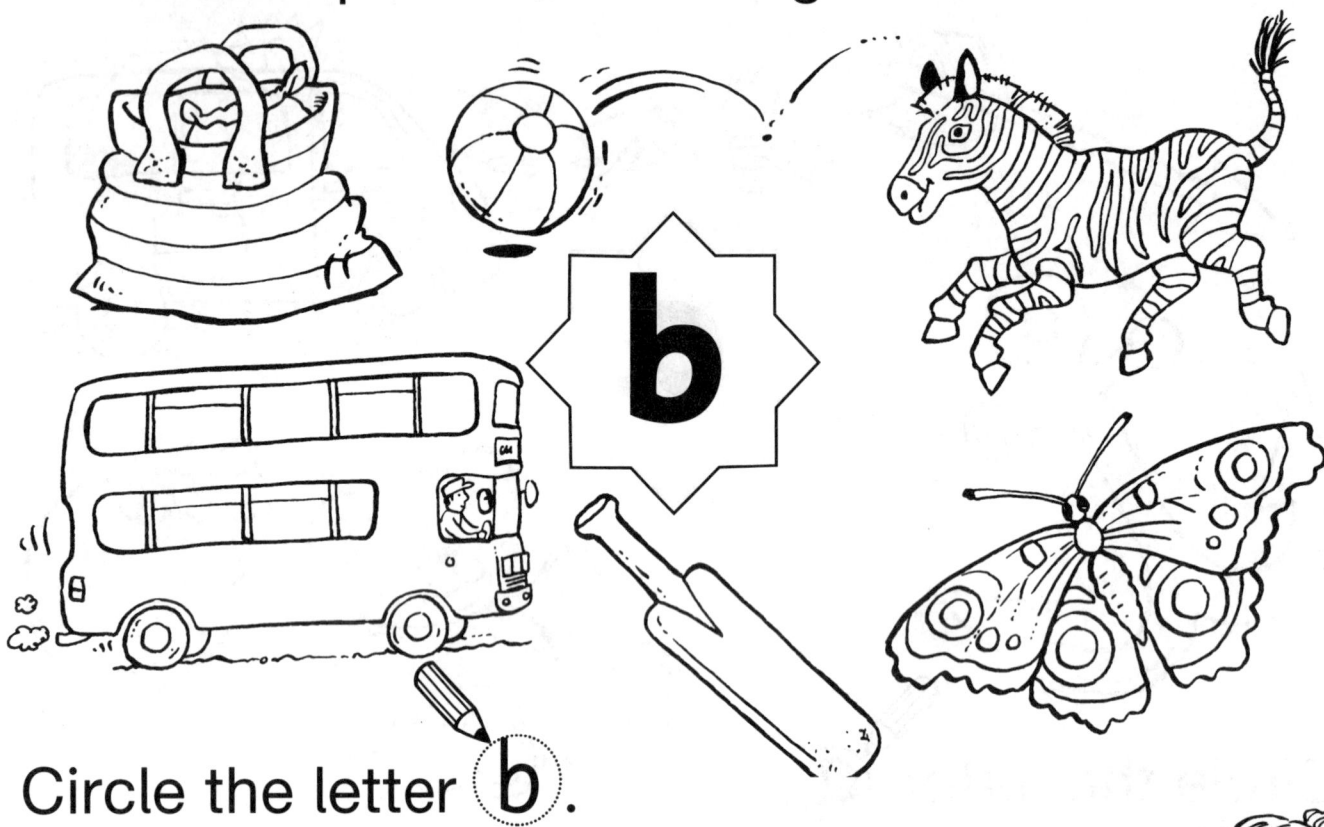

Circle the letter **b**.

a b c d e f g
h i j k l m
n o p q r s t
u v w x y z

Write the letter **b**.

Focus on Word Work © Louis Fidge and Sarah Lindsay, HarperCollins*Publishers* 1998

Name _____

COPYMASTER 3

Colour the pictures that begin with C.

Circle the letter C.

Write the letter C.

Name _____

COPYMASTER 4

Colour the pictures that begin with d.

Circle the letter d.

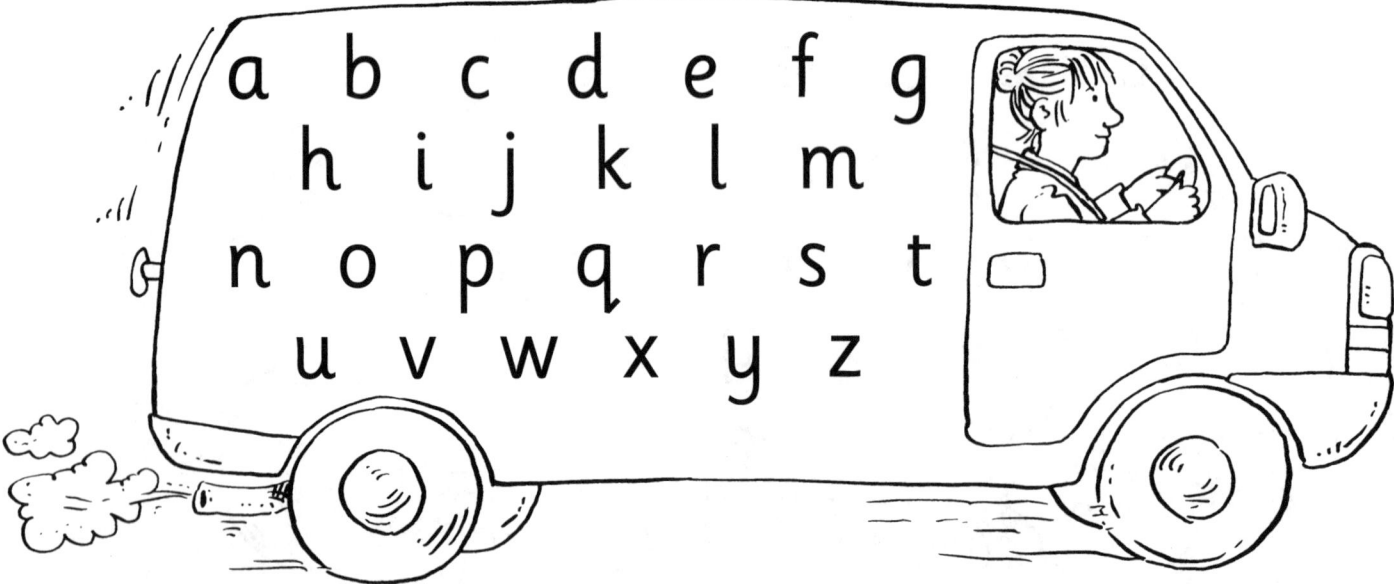

Write the letter d.

Focus on Word Work © Louis Fidge and Sarah Lindsay, HarperCollins Publishers 1998

Name _____

COPYMASTER 5

Colour the pictures that begin with *e*.

Circle the letter *e*.

a b c d e f g
h i j k l m
n o p q r s t
u v w x y z

Write the letter *e*.

Focus on Word Work © Louis Fidge and Sarah Lindsay, HarperCollins*Publishers* 1998

Name _____

COPYMASTER 6

Colour the pictures that begin with f.

Circle the letter f.

a b c d e f g
h i j k l m
n o p q r s t
u v w x y z

Write the letter f.

Focus on Word Work © Louis Fidge and Sarah Lindsay, **HarperCollins**Publishers 1998

Name _____

COPYMASTER
7

Colour the pictures that begin with g.

g

Circle the letter g.

a b c d e f g
h i j k l m
n o p q r s t
u v w x y z

Write the letter g.

Focus on Word Work © Louis Fidge and Sarah Lindsay, HarperCollins*Publishers* 1998

Name _____

COPYMASTER 8

Colour the pictures that begin with h.

Circle the letter h.

Write the letter h.

Name _____

COPYMASTER 9

Colour the pictures that begin with i.

Circle the letter i.

a b c d e f g
h i j k l m
n o p q r s t
u v w x y z

Write the letter i.

Focus on Word Work © Louis Fidge and Sarah Lindsay, HarperCollins*Publishers* 1998

Name _____

COPYMASTER 10

Colour the pictures that begin with j.

j

Circle the letter j.

a	b	c	d	e	f	g
h	i	j	k	l	m
n	o	p	q	r	s	t
u	v	w	x	y	z

Write the letter j.

Focus on Word Work © Louis Fidge and Sarah Lindsay, Harper**Collins**Publishers 1998

Name _____

COPYMASTER 11

Colour the pictures that begin with k.

k

Circle the letter k.

a b c d e f g
h i j k l m
n o p q r s t
u v w x y z

Write the letter k.

Focus on Word Work © Louis Fidge and Sarah Lindsay, HarperCollins*Publishers* 1998

Name _____

COPYMASTER 12

Colour the pictures that begin with l.

Circle the letter l.

a b c d e f g
h i j k l m
n o p q r s t
u v w x y z

Write the letter l.

Focus on Word Work © Louis Fidge and Sarah Lindsay, HarperCollins*Publishers* 1998

Name _____

COPYMASTER
13

Colour the pictures that begin with **m**.

Circle the letter **m**.

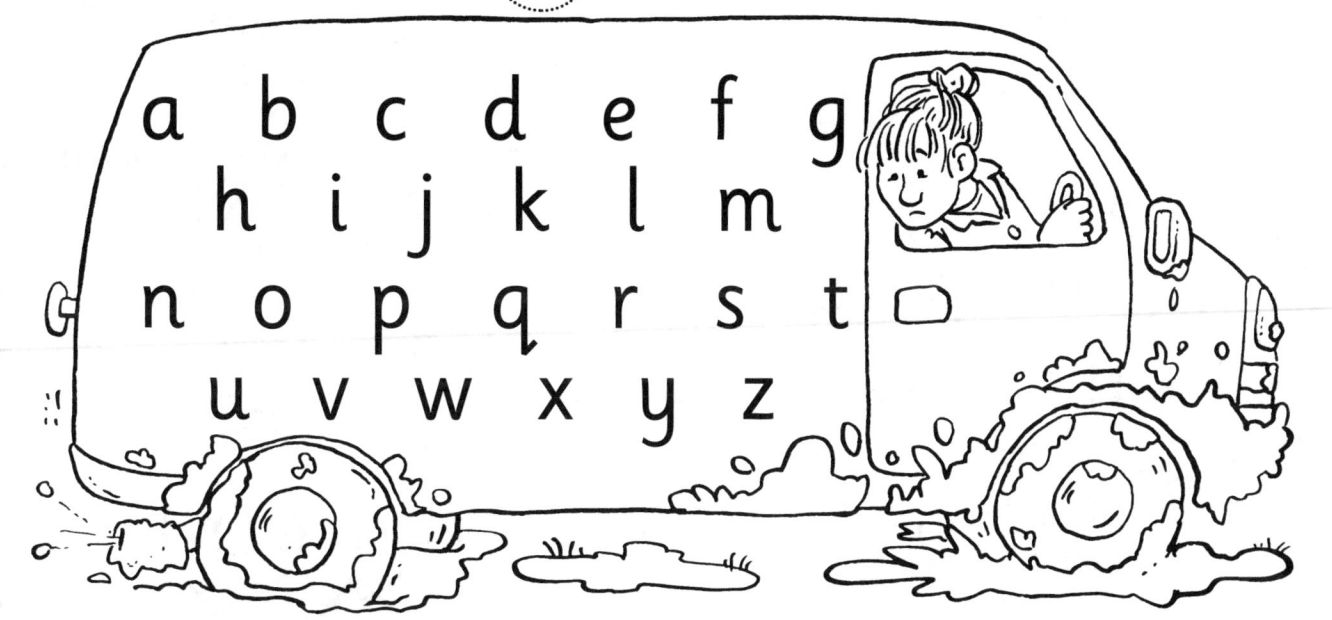

Write the letter **m**.

Focus on Word Work © Louis Fidge and Sarah Lindsay, HarperCollins Publishers 1998

Name _____

COPYMASTER
14

Colour the pictures that begin with n.

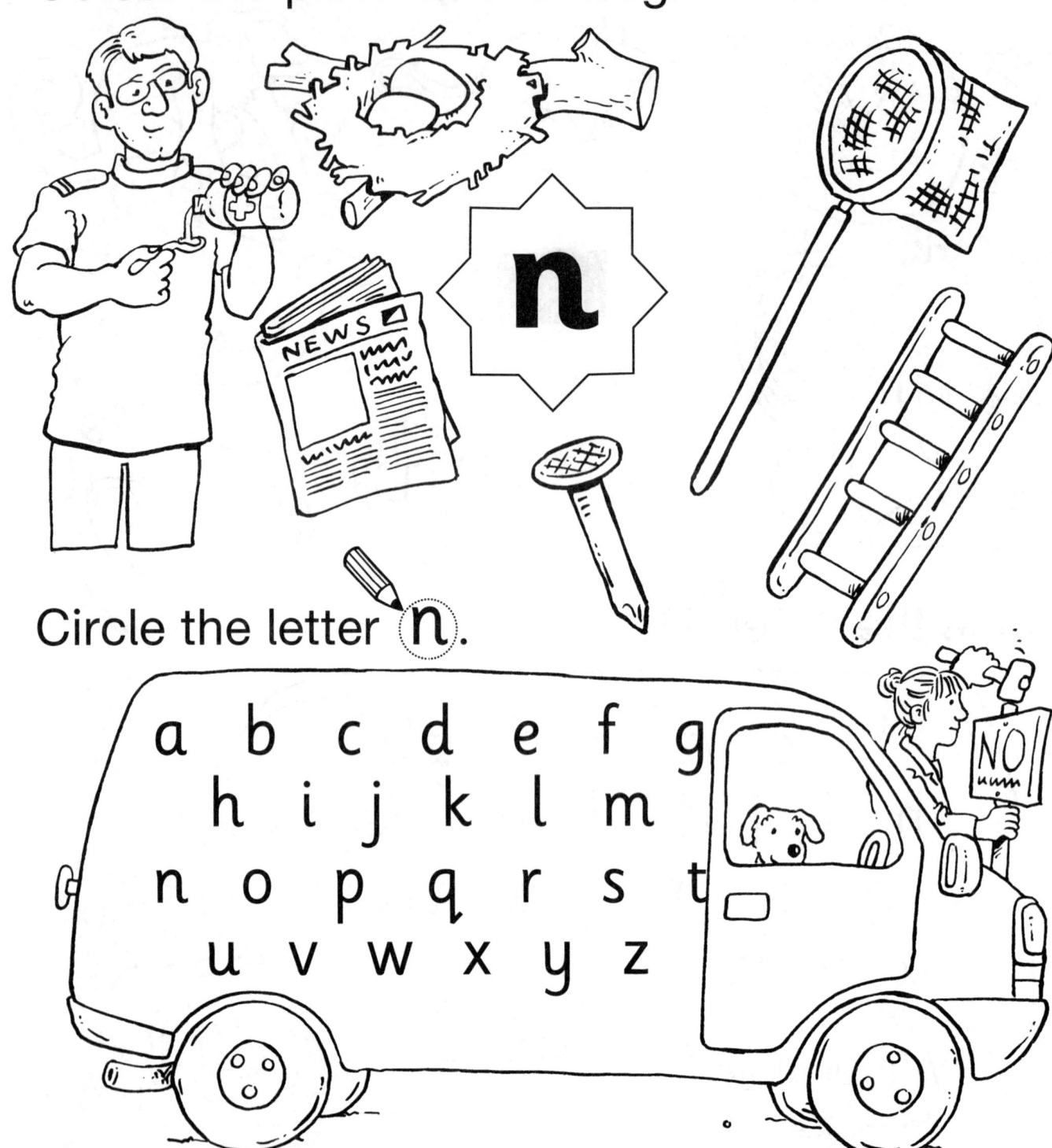

Circle the letter n.

Write the letter n.

Name _____

COPYMASTER 15

Colour the pictures that begin with O.

Circle the letter O.

a b c d e f g
h i j k l m
n o p q r s t
u v w x y z

Write the letter O.

Focus on Word Work © Louis Fidge and Sarah Lindsay, HarperCollins*Publishers* 1998

Name _____

COPYMASTER
16

Colour the pictures that begin with p.

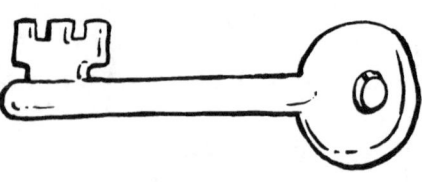

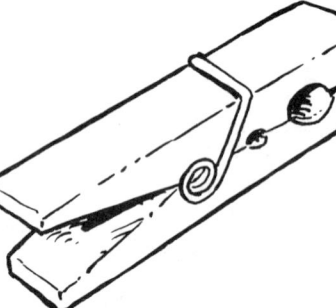

Circle the letter p.

a b c d e f g
h i j k l m
n o p q r s t
u v w x y z

Write the letter p.

Focus on Word Work © Louis Fidge and Sarah Lindsay, HarperCollins*Publishers* 1998

Name _____

COPYMASTER 17

Colour the pictures that begin with q.

q

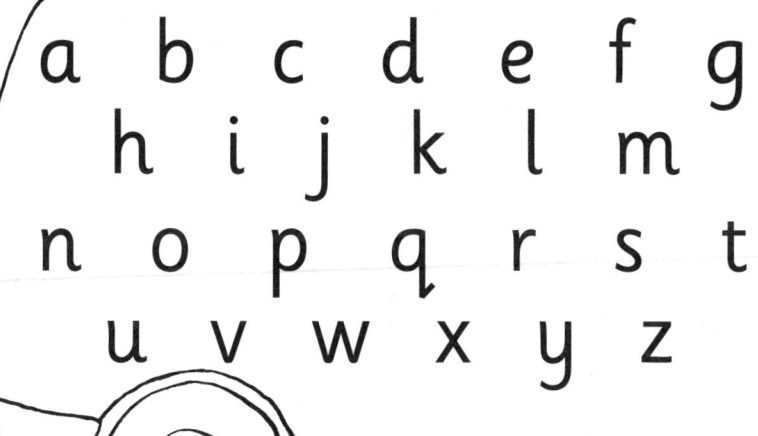

Circle the letter q.

a b c d e f g
h i j k l m
n o p q r s t
u v w x y z

Write the letter q.

Focus on Word Work © Louis Fidge and Sarah Lindsay, HarperCollins*Publishers* 1998

Name _____

COPYMASTER
18

Colour the pictures that begin with r.

Circle the letter r.

a b c d e f g
h i j k l m
n o p q r s t
u v w x y z

Write the letter r.

Focus on Word Work © Louis Fidge and Sarah Lindsay, HarperCollins*Publishers* 1998

Name _____

COPYMASTER
19

Colour the pictures that begin with **S**.

Circle the letter **S**.

a b c d e f g
h i j k l m
n o p q r s t
u v w x y z

Write the letter **S**.

Focus on Word Work © Louis Fidge and Sarah Lindsay, HarperCollins*Publishers* 1998

Name _____

COPYMASTER
20

Colour the pictures that begin with t.

Circle the letter t.

a b c d e f g
h i j k l m
n o p q r s t
u v w x y z

Write the letter t.

Focus on Word Work © Louis Fidge and Sarah Lindsay, HarperCollins*Publishers* 1998

Name _____

COPYMASTER
21

Colour the pictures that begin with u.

u

up

under

Circle the letter u.

a b c d e f g
h i j k l m
n o p q r s t
u v w x y z

Write the letter u.

u

Focus on Word Work © Louis Fidge and Sarah Lindsay, HarperCollins*Publishers* 1998

Name _____

COPYMASTER
22

Colour the pictures that begin with **V**.

Circle the letter **V**.

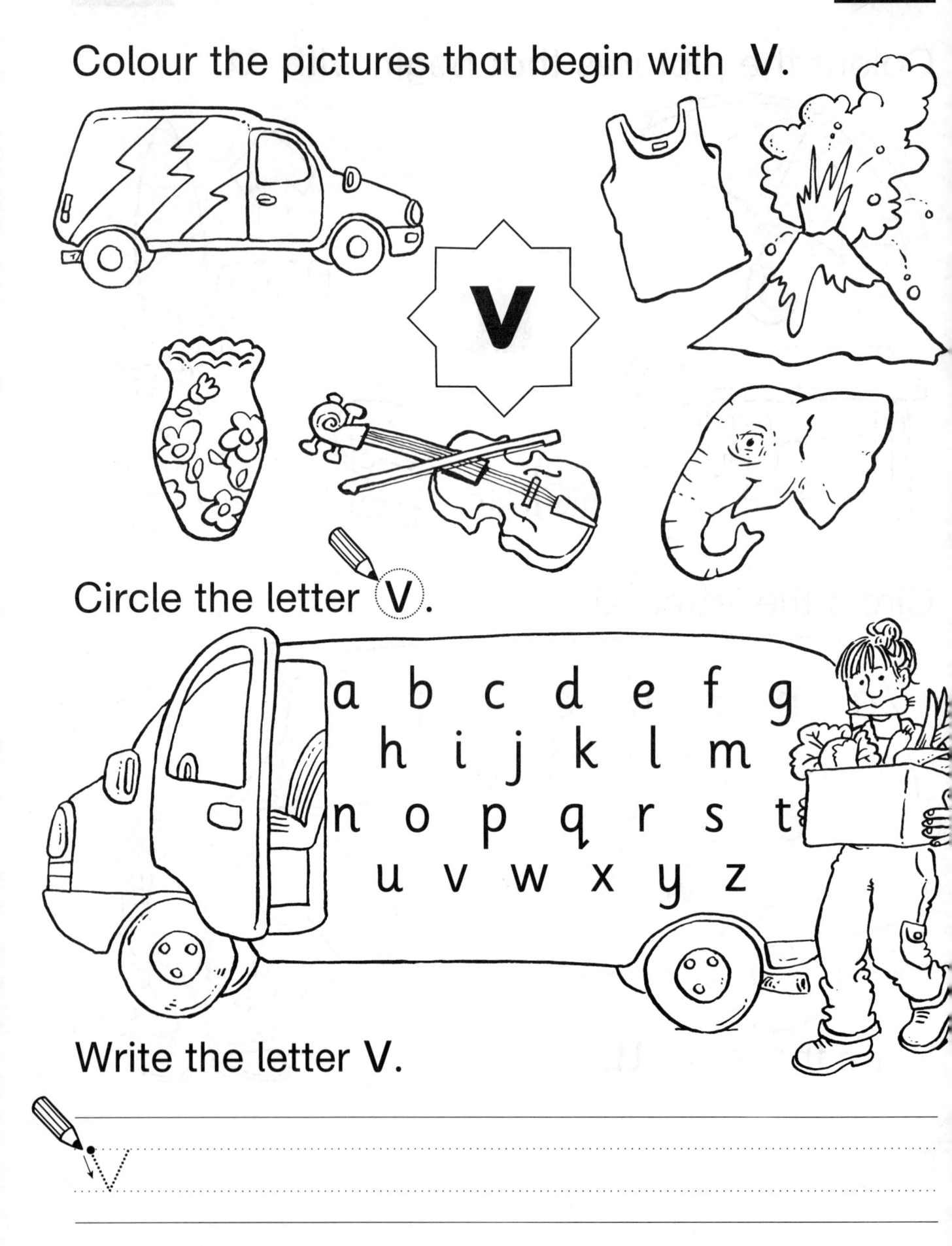

a b c d e f g
h i j k l m
n o p q r s t
u v w x y z

Write the letter **V**.

Focus on Word Work © Louis Fidge and Sarah Lindsay, HarperCollins*Publishers* 1998

Name _____

COPYMASTER 23

Colour the pictures that begin with W.

Circle the letter W.

Write the letter W.

Focus on Word Work © Louis Fidge and Sarah Lindsay, HarperCollins*Publishers* 1998

Name _____

COPYMASTER 24

Colour the pictures that end with X.

Circle the letter X.

Write the letter X.

Name _____

COPYMASTER
25

Colour the pictures that begin with y.

Circle the letter y.

Write the letter y.

Focus on Word Work © Louis Fidge and Sarah Lindsay, HarperCollins*Publishers* 1998

Name _____

COPYMASTER 26

Colour the pictures that begin with Z.

Circle the letter Z.

a b c d e f g
h i j k l m
n o p q r s t
u v w x y z

Write the letter Z.

Focus on Word Work © Louis Fidge and Sarah Lindsay, HarperCollins Publishers 1998

Name _____

COPYMASTER
27

| a c h t |

Write the correct letter.

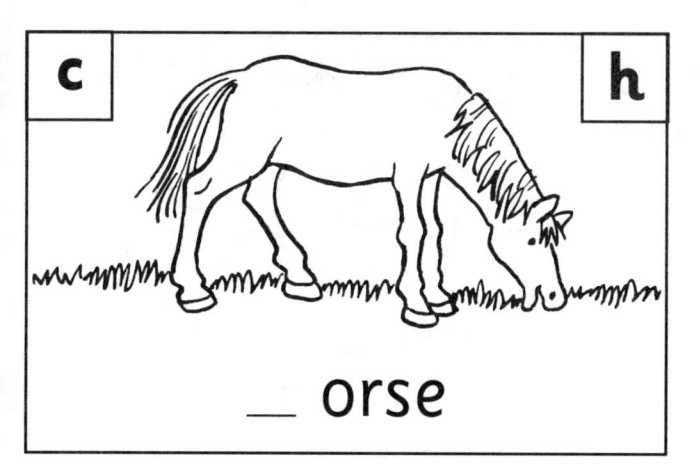

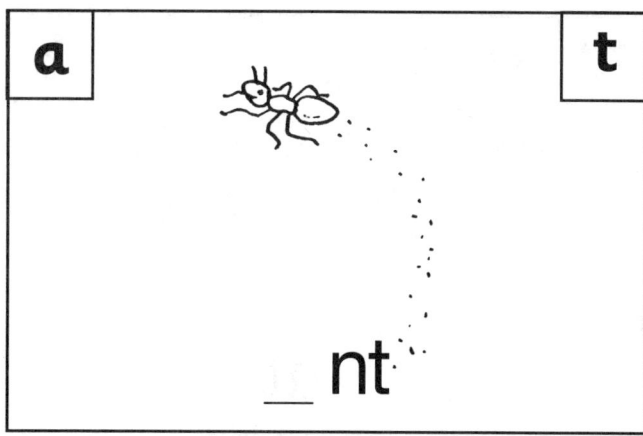

a | c
_at

h | t
_iger

c | h
_orse

a | t
_nt

Write the words.

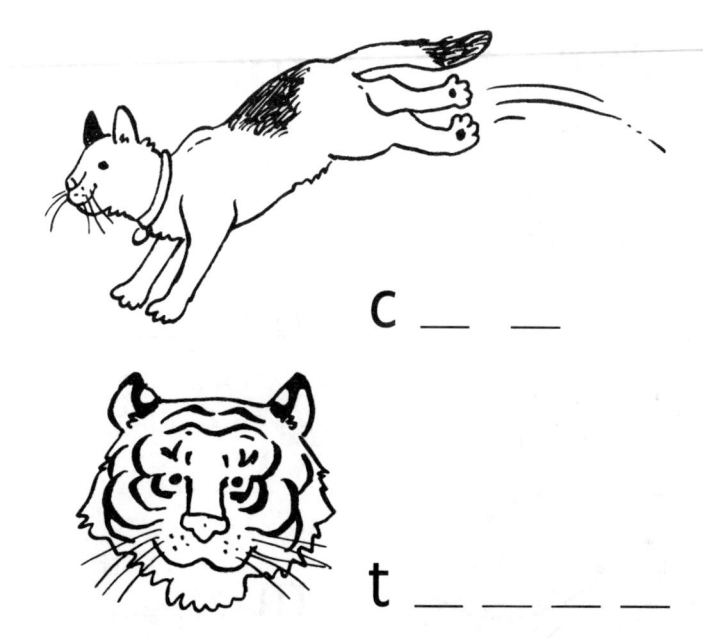

a _ _

c _ _

h _ _ _ _

t _ _ _ _ _

Unit 1 Now try these   *Focus on Word Work* © Louis Fidge and Sarah Lindsay, HarperCollins*Publishers* 1998

Name _____

COPYMASTER 28

| b l m s |

Write the correct letter.

b		l
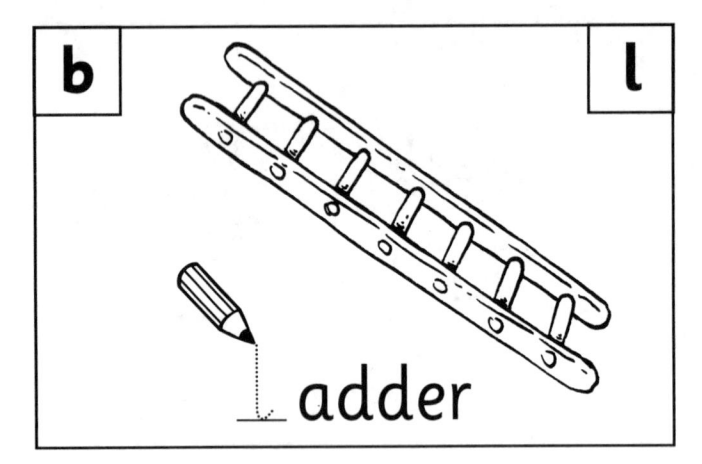	_adder	

m		s
	_oon	

m		b
	_at	

s		l
	_un	

Write the words.

b _ _

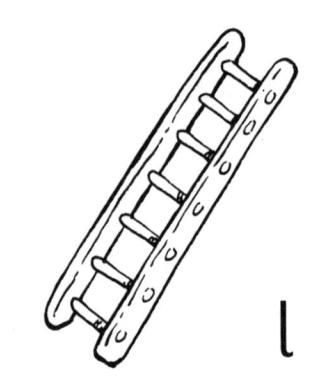

l _ _ _ _ _

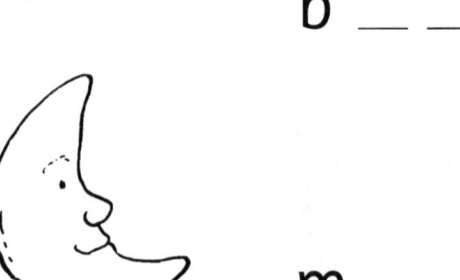

m _ _ _

s _ _

Unit 2 Now try these   Focus on Word Work © Louis Fidge and Sarah Lindsay, HarperCollins Publishers 1998

Name _____

COPYMASTER
29

g i n p

Write the correct letter.

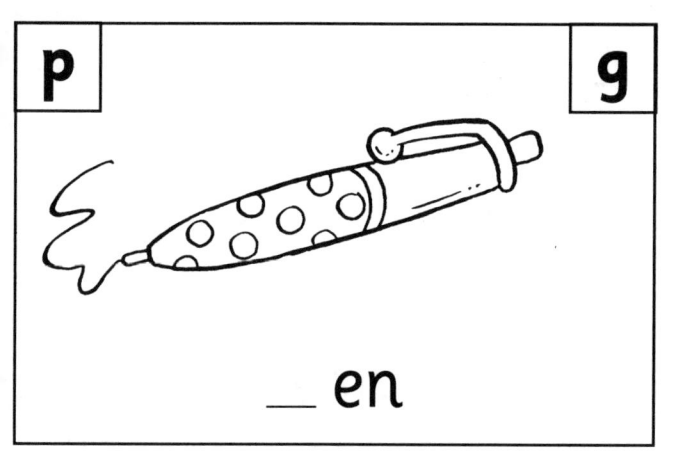

g		i
	girl	

n		p
	_ urse	

p		g
	_ en	

n		i
	_ nk	

Write the words.

g _ _ _

i _ _

n _ _ _ _

p _ _

Unit 3 Now try these   Focus on Word Work © Louis Fidge and Sarah Lindsay, HarperCollins*Publishers* 1998

Name _____

COPYMASTER 30

| d e f r |

Write the correct letter.

d		e
	_gg	

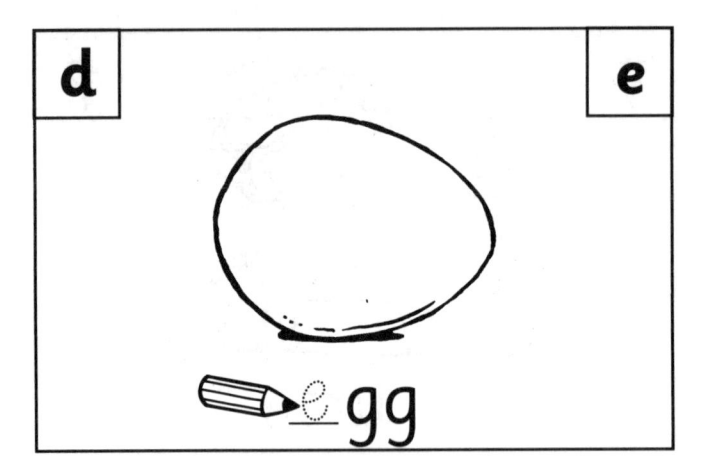

f		r
	_ at	

e		f
	_ ish	

d		r
	_ onkey	

Write the words.

d _ _ _ _ _ _

e _ _

f _ _ _

r _ _

Unit 4 Now try these   Focus on Word Work © Louis Fidge and Sarah Lindsay, HarperCollins*Publishers* 1998

Name _____

COPYMASTER
31

k o v y

Write the correct letter.

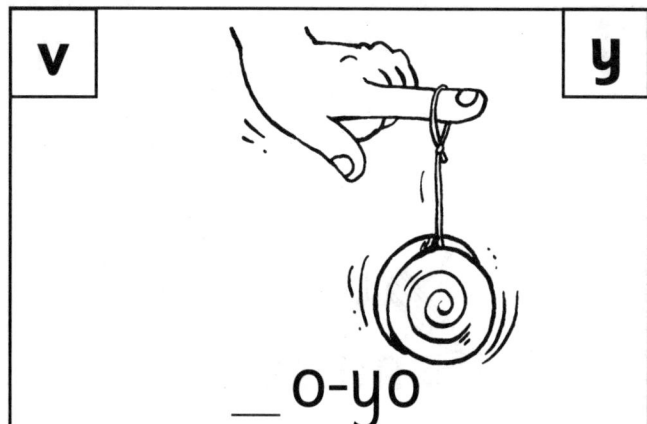

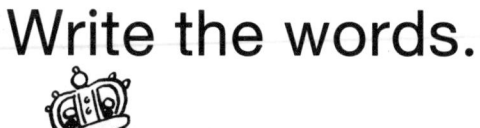

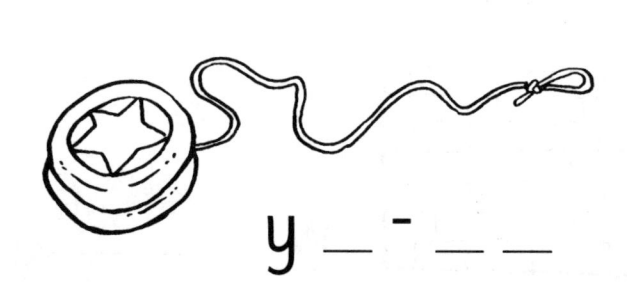

k ... o	v ... y
_ctopus	_o-yo

o ... v	k ... y
_an	_ing

Write the words.

k _ _ _   o _ _ _ _ _ _

v _ _   y _ - _ _

Unit 5 Now try these   *Focus on Word Work* © Louis Fidge and Sarah Lindsay, HarperCollins*Publishers* 1998

Name _____

COPYMASTER
32

| j u w |

Write the correct letter.

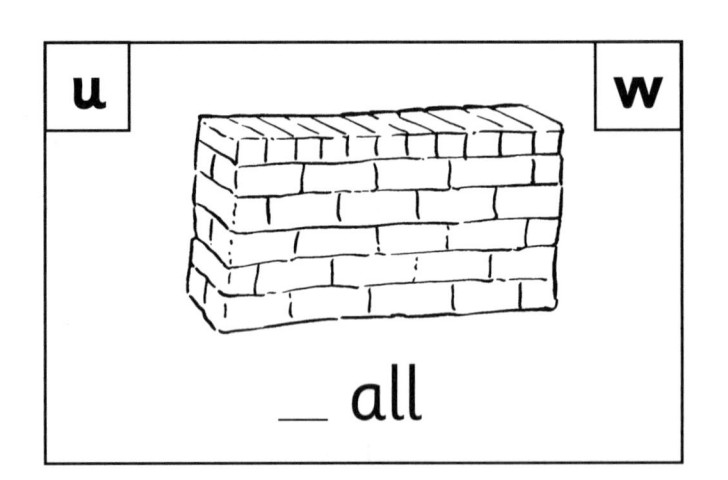

| j | [umbrella] | u |
| _ mbrella |

| w | [jug] | j |
| _ ug |

| u | [wall] | w |
| _ all |

Write the words.

[jug] j _ _

[umbrella] u _ _ _ _ _ _

[wall] w _ _ _

Unit 6 Now try these   Focus on Word Work © Louis Fidge and Sarah Lindsay, HarperCollins Publishers 1998

Name _____

COPYMASTER 33

q x z

Write the correct letter.

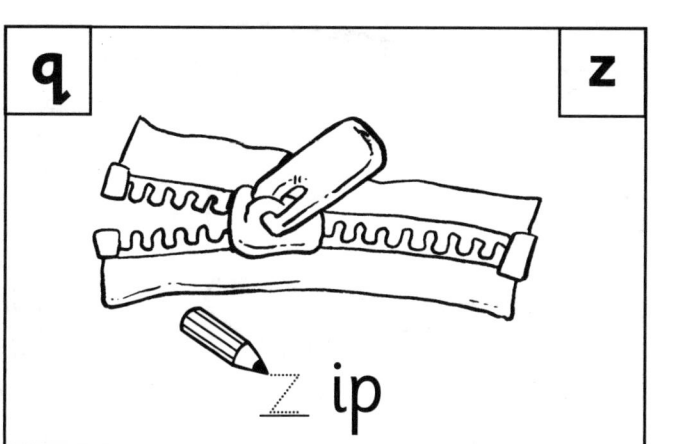

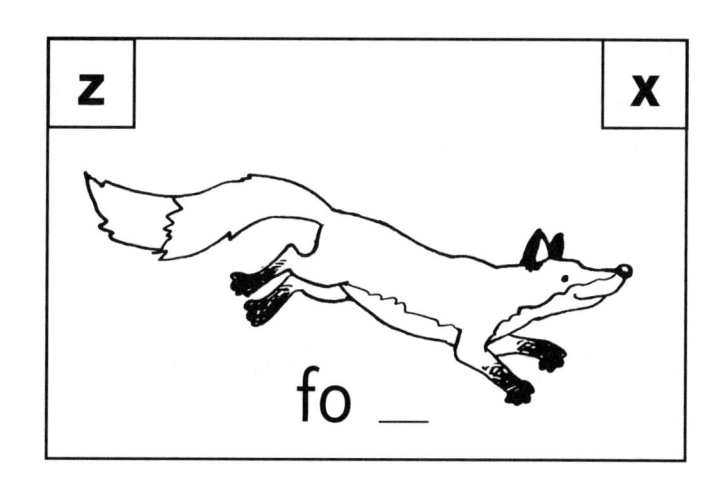

q	z
_ip	

x	q
_ueen	

z	x
fo _	

Write the words.

q _ _ _ _ _

z _ _ _

_ _ x

Unit 7 Now try these   Focus on Word Work © Louis Fidge and Sarah Lindsay, HarperCollinsPublishers 1998

Name _____

COPYMASTER 34

Capital letters

Fill in the missing capital or lower case letters.

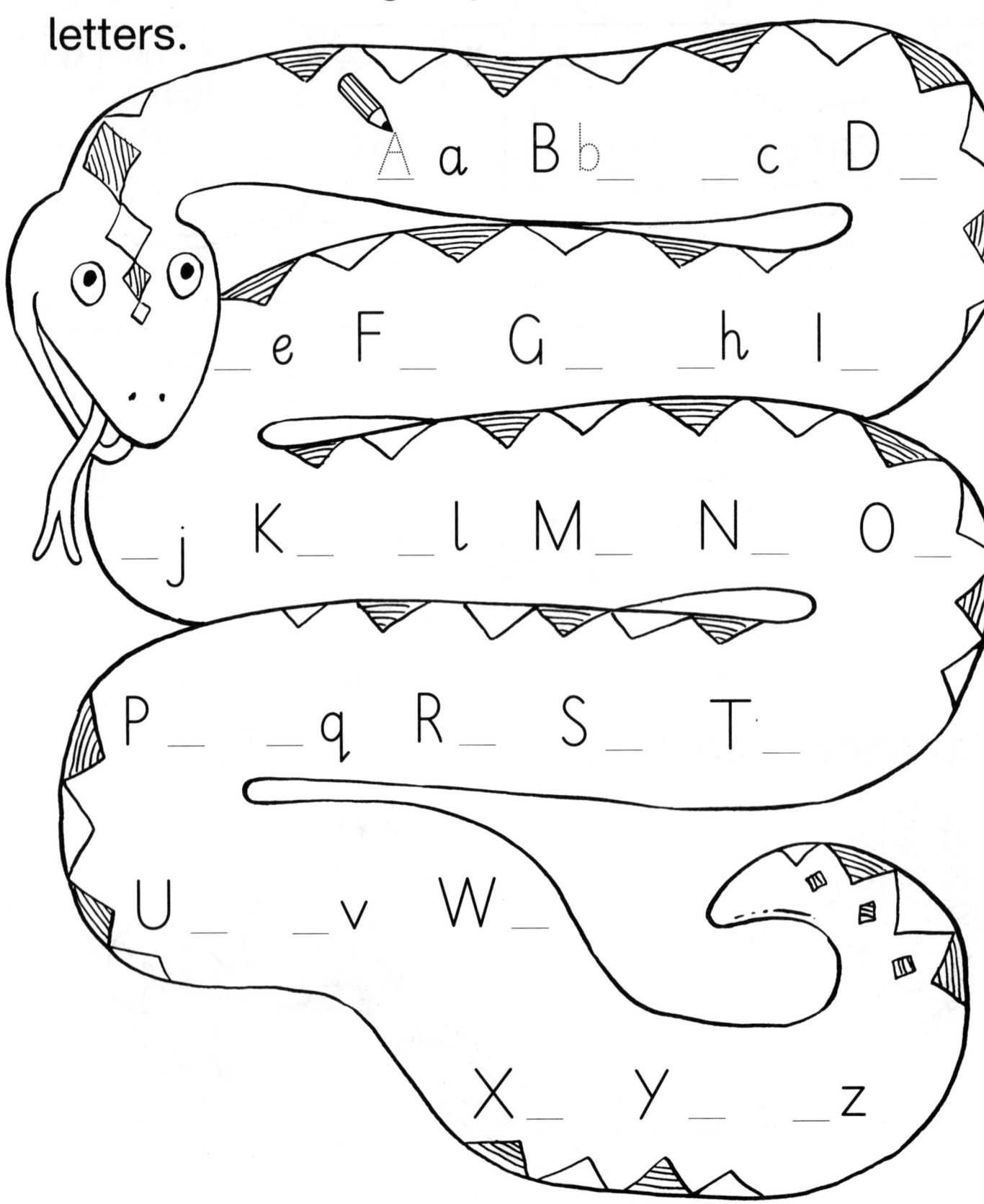

A a B b _ c D _

_ e F _ G _ _ h I _

_ j K _ _ l M _ N _ O _

P _ _ q R _ S _ T _

U _ _ v W _

X _ Y _ _ z

Unit 8 Now try these   Focus on Word Work © Louis Fidge and Sarah Lindsay, HarperCollins *Publishers* 1998

Name _____

COPYMASTER
35

Word building 1

Write the words.   Label the pictures.

v→an _van_

m→an _____

f→an _____

p→an _____

b→in _____

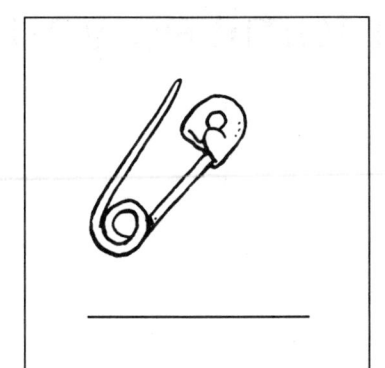

t→in _____

p→in _____

w→in _____

Unit 9 Now try these   Focus on Word Work © Louis Fidge and Sarah Lindsay, HarperCollins*Publishers* 1998

Name _____

COPYMASTER
36

Word families

Cross out the odd word in each line.

1. ham   jam   p~~a~~t   ram
2. ten   red   men   pen
3. fit   sit   pit   big
4. pop   hop   fox   top
5. bug   dug   hug   cup

Write the word families you found.

1. ham   jam   ram
2. ____   ____   ____
3. ____   ____   ____
4. ____   ____   ____
5. ____   ____   ____

Unit 10 Now try these   Focus on Word Work © Louis Fidge and Sarah Lindsay, HarperCollins Publishers 1998

Rhyming words

Choose a word to fill each gap.

1. ran   van   man

The _man_ _____ to his _____ .

2. pop   shop   hop

I can _____ and _____ into the _____ .

3. tub   Rub   dub

_____ a dub _____ , three men in a _____ .

Name _____

sh ch

Choose **sh** or **ch** to fill each gap.

_sh_ ip   _ _ at   _ _ op

bun _ _   _ _ ed   fi _ _

Write the words.

sh _ _   ch _ _

sh _ _   ch _ _

_ _ sh   _ _ _ ch

COPYMASTER 38

Unit 12 Now try these   *Focus on Word Work* © Louis Fidge and Sarah Lindsay, HarperCollins*Publishers* 1998

Final letter sounds

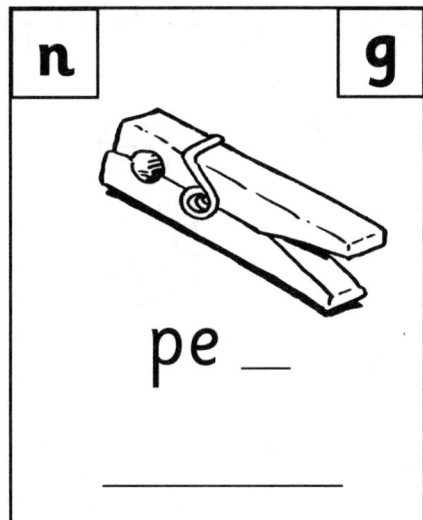

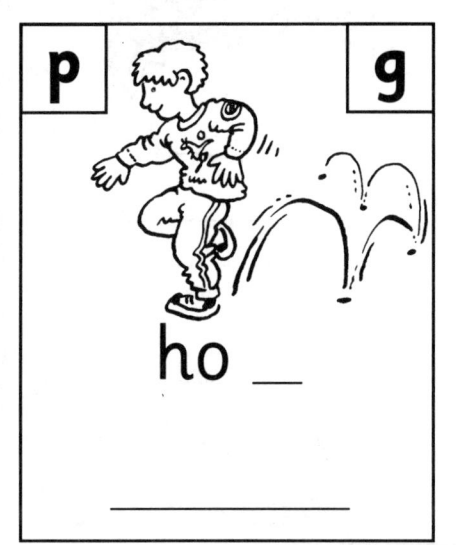

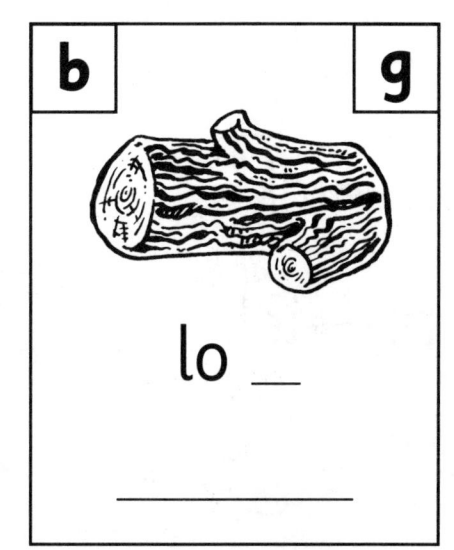

n / t	n / g	t / x
fan / fan	pe _	si _

p / g	n / p	m / d
ho _	su _	sa _

g / d	t / n	b / g
be _	bi _	lo _

COPYMASTER 40

Name _____

Word building 2

Write the words.   Label the pictures.

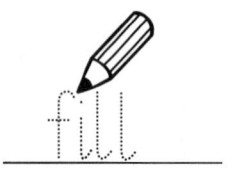

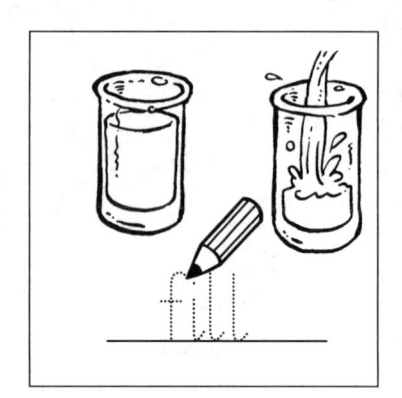

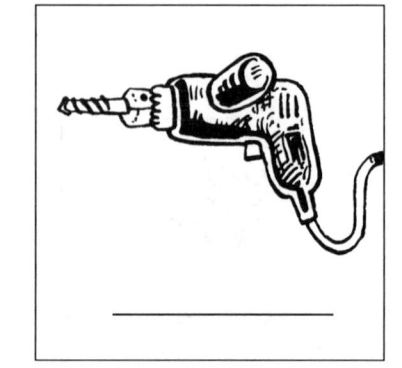

f→ill   fill

p→ill   _____

sp→ill _____

dr→ill _____

s→ick   _____

l→ick   _____

fl→ick _____

br→ick _____

Unit 14 Now try these   *Focus on Word Work* © Louis Fidge and Sarah Lindsay, HarperCollins*Publishers* 1998

Name _____

COPYMASTER 41

th

a **th**ick pizza    a **th**in pizza

Write the words.

thin   __ick   __ink
thin   _____   _____

ba __   pa __   mo __
_____   _____   _____

Label each picture.

thick   _____   _____

_____   _____   _____

Focus on Word Work © Louis Fidge and Sarah Lindsay, HarperCollins*Publishers* 1998

Name _____

COPYMASTER
42

High frequency words checklist (Year R)

I	he	away	dog	went
up	is	play	big	was
look	said	a	my	of
we	go	am	mum	me
like	you	cat	no	she
and	are	to	dad	see
on	this	come	all	it
at	going	day	get	yes
for	they	the	in	can

Focus on Word Work © Louis Fidge and Sarah Lindsay, HarperCollins*Publishers* 1998

Name _____

COPYMASTER 43

High frequency words lotto cards

I	up	look	we	like
and	on	at	for	he
is	said	go	you	are

this	going	they	away	play
a	am	cat	to	come
day	the	dog	big	my

mum	no	dad	all	get
in	went	was	of	me
she	see	it	yes	can

Focus on Word Work © Louis Fidge and Sarah Lindsay, HarperCollins*Publishers* 1998

Name _____

COPYMASTER 44

High frequency words lotto cards

away	up	big	said	of
am	like	no	are	see
come	at	get	they	can

dog	is	was	a	we
mum	you	she	to	on
all	going	yes	the	he

I	went	play	look	my
go	me	cat	and	dad
this	it	day	for	in

Focus on Word Work © Louis Fidge and Sarah Lindsay, HarperCollins*Publishers* 1998

Name _____

COPYMASTER 45

High frequency words lotto cards

I	away	went	up	play
was	look	a	of	we
am	like	me	cat	she

and	to	see	on	come
all	at	day	yes	for
the	can	he	dog	is

big	said	my	go	mum
you	no	are	dad	this
it	going	get	they	in

Focus on Word Work © Louis Fidge and Sarah Lindsay, HarperCollinsPublishers 1998

Name _____   COPYMASTER 46

High frequency words lotto cards

went	big	a	go	like
dog	play	said	we	look
is	away	up	I	he

and	you	am	my	was
on	are	cat	mum	of
at	this	to	no	me

for	going	come	dad	she
they	day	all	see	can
in	yes	it	get	the

Focus on Word Work © Louis Fidge and Sarah Lindsay, HarperCollinsPublishers 1998

Name _____

COPYMASTER 47

High frequency words game

Play the game.

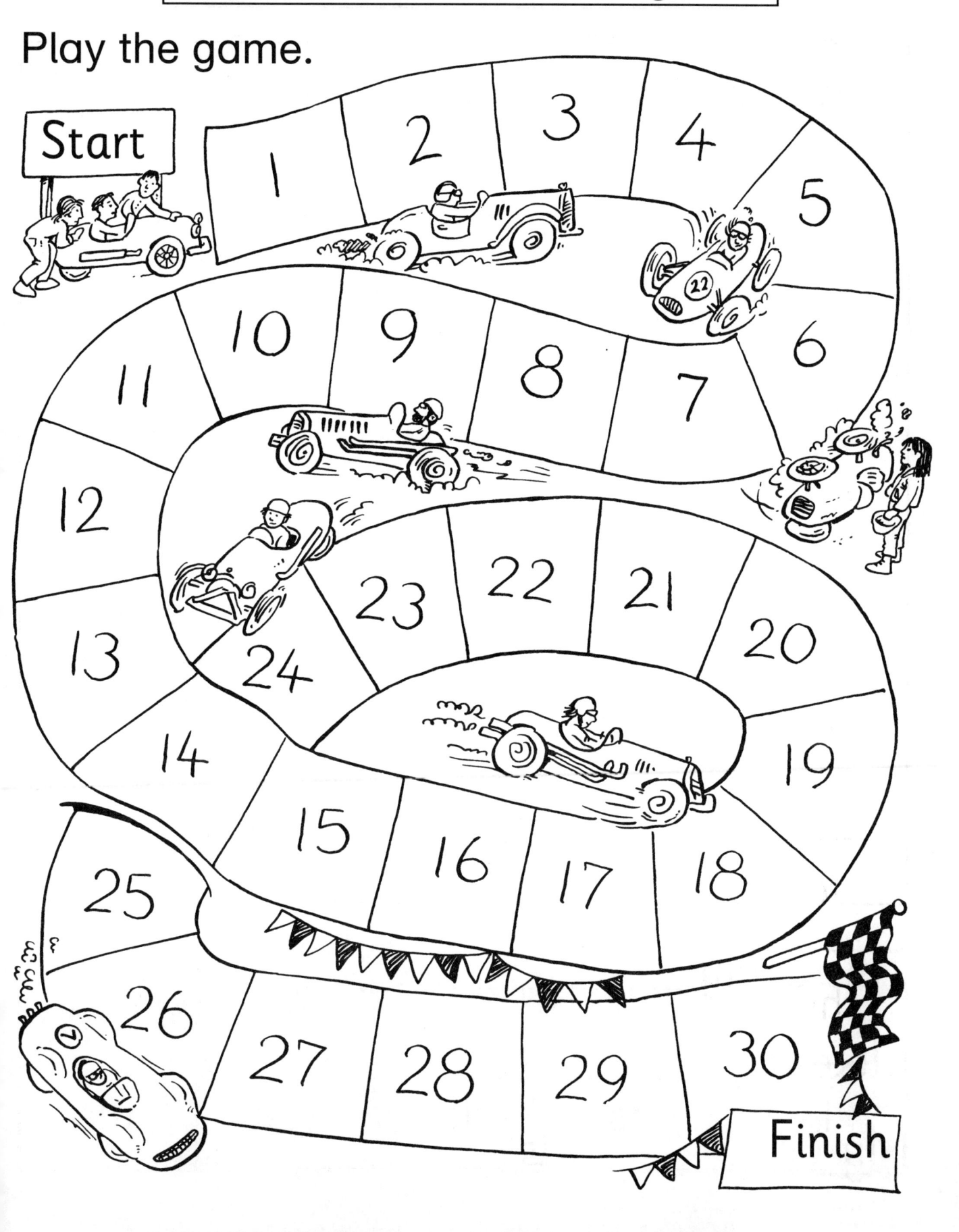

Start

1 2 3 4 5 6 7 8 9 10 11 12 13 14 15 16 17 18 19 20 21 22 23 24 25 26 27 28 29 30

Finish

Focus on Word Work © Louis Fidge and Sarah Lindsay, HarperCollins*Publishers* 1998

Name _____

COPYMASTER 48

Using high frequency words

This is my _____ .

I like my _____ .

My _____ is _____ .

Focus on Word Work © Louis Fidge and Sarah Lindsay, HarperCollins*Publishers* 1998

Name _____

COPYMASTER 49

Using high frequency words

This is a _____ .

This is a _____ .

This is a _____ and a _____ .

Focus on Word Work © Louis Fidge and Sarah Lindsay, HarperCollins*Publishers* 1998

Name _____

COPYMASTER 50

Using high frequency words

Copy and complete each sentence.
Draw the pictures.

I can see _____.
I can see _____.

I like _____.
_____.

I went to _____.
_____.

I can see _____.
_____.

I am a _____.
_____.

Focus on Word Work © Louis Fidge and Sarah Lindsay, **HarperCollins**Publishers 1998

Name _____

COPYMASTER 51

Writing high frequency words

Read the words.
Circle the parts that are the same.
Cover the words.
Write the words without copying.

he	he
me	
we	
she	

no	
go	
to	

the	
they	
this	

day	
away	
play	

Focus on Word Work © Louis Fidge and Sarah Lindsay, HarperCollins Publishers 1998

Name _____

COPYMASTER 52

Writing high frequency words

Look at the high frequency word checklist.
Write some words beginning with:

a _am_ _____

g _____

i _____

l _____

o _____

s _____

t _____

w _____

y _____

Focus on Word Work © Louis Fidge and Sarah Lindsay, HarperCollins*Publishers* 1998

Name _____

COPYMASTER
53

Writing high frequency words

Look at the high frequency word checklist. Write two words which have only one letter.

_____ _____

Write five words which have two letters.

_____ _____ _____ _____ _____

Write ten words which have three letters.

_____ _____ _____ _____ _____

_____ _____ _____ _____ _____

Write five words which have four letters.

_____ _____ _____ _____ _____

Write one word which has five letters.

_____

Focus on Word Work © Louis Fidge and Sarah Lindsay, HarperCollins*Publishers* 1998

Name _____

COPYMASTER
54

The alphabet

Underline the first letter of each word.
Write the words in alphabetical order.

sit   **h**it   hit   sit

bat   **m**at   _____   _____

ten   **p**en   _____   _____

yell   **s**ell   _____   _____

net   **w**et   _____   _____

pan   **r**an   _____   _____

dog   **l**og   _____   _____

Unit 1 Now try these   *Focus on Word Work* © Louis Fidge and Sarah Lindsay, HarperCollins*Publishers* 1998

COPYMASTER
55

Name _____

Non-rhyming words

Write a word to match the picture.
Use one letter from each column.

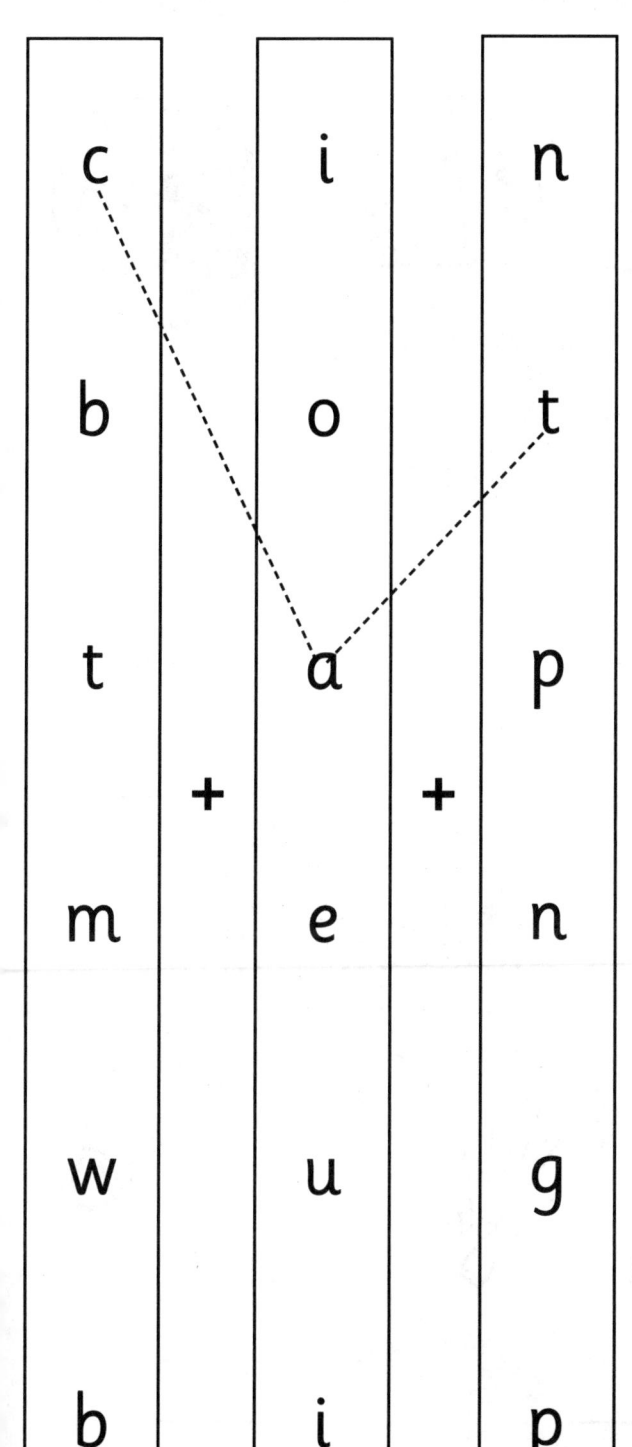

c	i	n
b	o	t
t	a	p
+	+	
m	e	n
w	u	g
b	i	p

1. cat 
2. _____ 
3. _____ 
4. _____ 
5. _____ 
6. _____

Unit 2 Now try these   Focus on Word Work © Louis Fidge and Sarah Lindsay, HarperCollins Publishers 1998

Name _____

COPYMASTER
56

Rhyming words

Write two more rhyming words.
Use the pictures to help you.

hat   jug   wet

___   ___   ___

___   ___   ___

tin   pan   hot

___   ___   ___

___   ___   ___

Unit 3 Now try these   Focus on Word Work © Louis Fidge and Sarah Lindsay, HarperCollins Publishers 1998

Name _____

COPYMASTER 57

ff ll ss

Choose a word to fill each gap.

| press   sniff   fell   bell   mess   doll |

1. I _____ when I have a cold.

2. I hear the school _____ at the end of lunch.

3. I make a _____ when I paint.

4. I _____ on the ground.

5. I played with my _____.

6. I had to _____ the bell.

Unit 4 Now try these   Focus on Word Work © Louis Fidge and Sarah Lindsay, HarperCollins*Publishers* 1998

COPYMASTER
58

Name _____

ng nk

1. Choose the ending. Write the word.

ba nk   bank

si __ __   _____

wi __ __   _____

wi __ __   _____

ba __ __   _____

2. Write four words that end in **ng** or **nk**.

_____ _____ _____ _____

Unit 5 Now try these   Focus on Word Work © Louis Fidge and Sarah Lindsay, HarperCollins Publishers 1998

Name _____

COPYMASTER 59

| fl tr |

1. Join the letters to make some words.

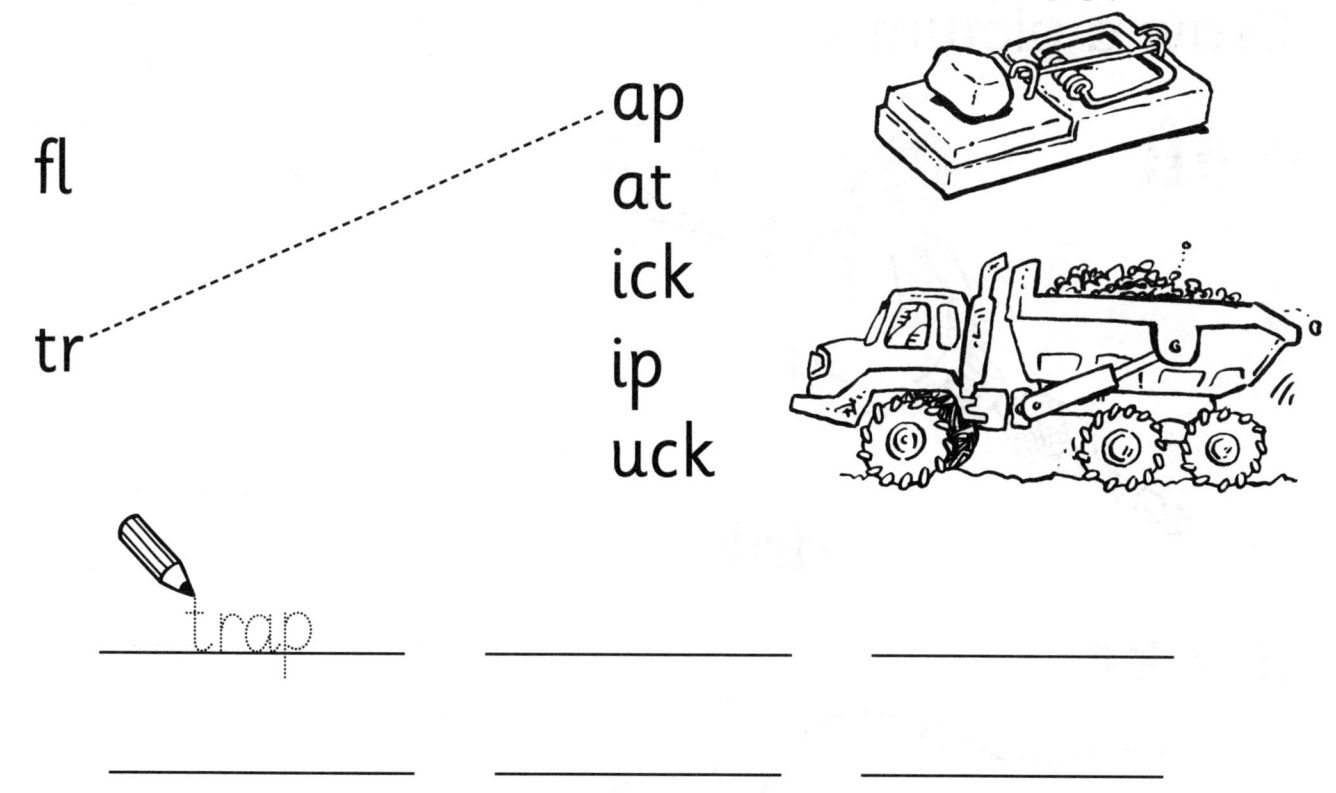

fl   ap
            at
tr   ick
            ip
            uck

trap _____ _____

_____ _____ _____

_____ _____

Can you find eight words?

2. Write another word that begins with **fl**. _____

3. Write another word that begins with **tr**. _____

Unit 6 Now try these   *Focus on Word Work* © Louis Fidge and Sarah Lindsay, HarperCollins*Publishers* 1998

Name _____

COPYMASTER 60

Spelling patterns

Write a word with the same pattern.
Draw a picture.

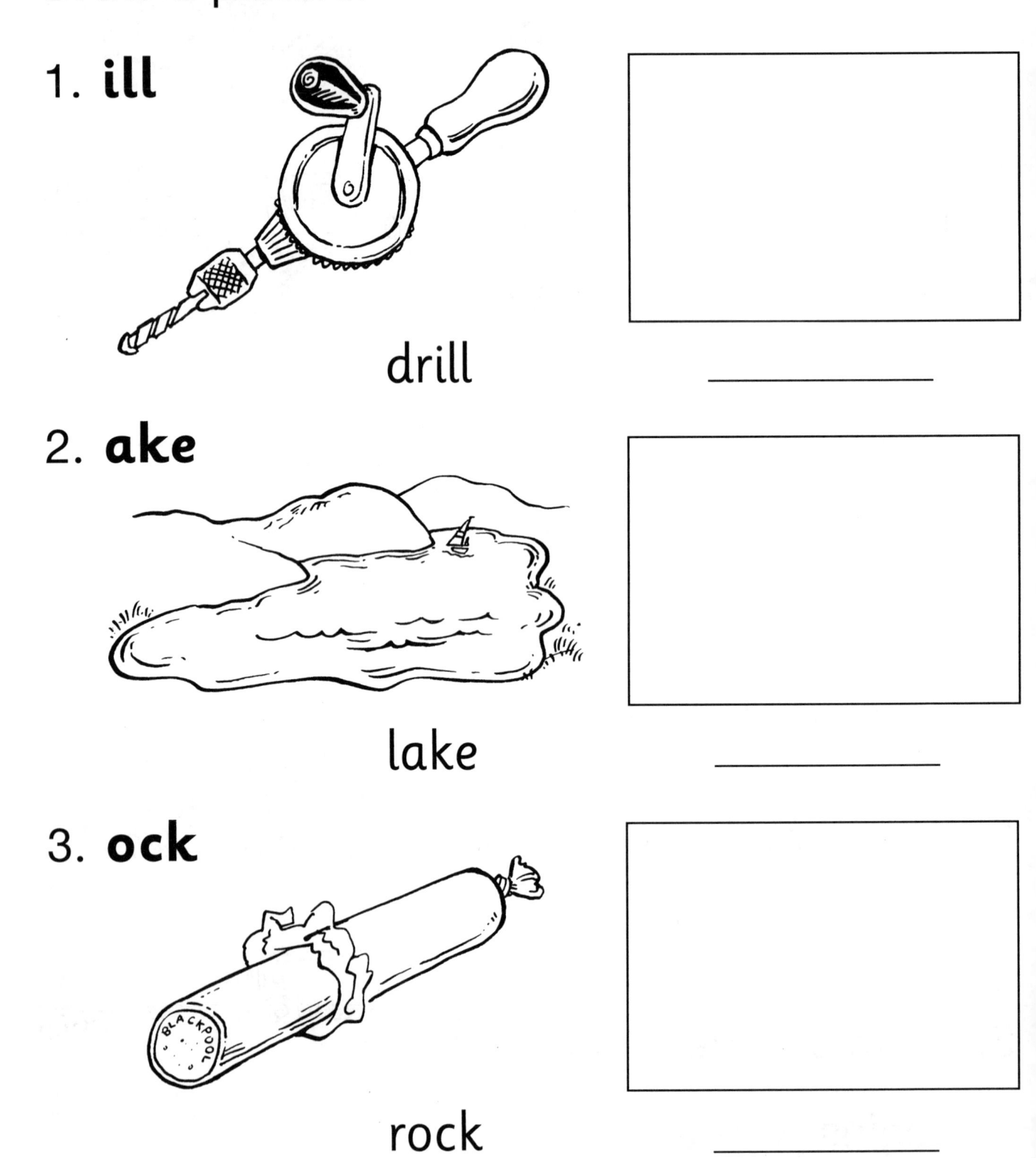

1. **ill**

   drill

2. **ake**

   lake

3. **ock**

   rock

Unit 7 Now try these   Focus on Word Work © Louis Fidge and Sarah Lindsay, HarperCollins*Publishers* 1998

Name _____

COPYMASTER
61

nd st

1. Choose the ending. Write the word.

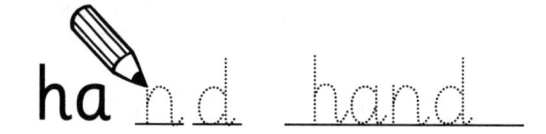

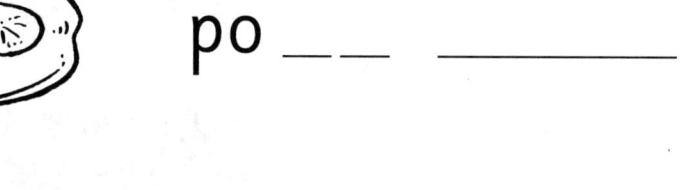

ha nd hand

po ___ _____

fi ___ _____

du ___ _____

be ___ _____

2. Write four more words that end in **nd** or **st**.

_____ _____ _____ _____

Unit 8 Now try these — Focus on Word Work © Louis Fidge and Sarah Lindsay, HarperCollins Publishers 1998

Name _____

COPYMASTER 62

Plurals

Fill the gaps.

1 one	**2** two	**3** three	**4** four	**5** five
6 six	**7** seven	**8** eight	**9** nine	**10** ten

one   **plural**

1. one duck   _____ ducks

2. one cow   two _____

3. ____ bird   six birds

4. one _____   three frogs

5. ____ cat   five cats

6. one goat   three _____

7. one dog   _____ dogs

8. ____ hen   ten hens

Unit 9 Now try these   *Focus on Word Work* © Louis Fidge and Sarah Lindsay, HarperCollins*Publishers* 1998

Name _____

COPYMASTER 63

ee oo

1. Look at the endings. Write the words in the table.

seed	boot	fool	jeep
hoot	sleep	pool	feed
sheep	weed	speed	shoot
root	deep	tool	stool

eed	**eep**	**ool**	**oot**
seed			

2. Add one more word to each column.

Unit 10 Now try these   Focus on Word Work © Louis Fidge and Sarah Lindsay, HarperCollins Publishers 1998

Name _____

COPYMASTER 64

oa ai

Choose a word to answer the clue. Write the word.

| goat   snail   foal   nail   toad   rain |

What am I?

1. I carry my house on my back. _snail_

2. I look like a frog. _____

3. I am hit with a hammer. _____

4. I am a baby horse. _____

5. My baby is called a kid. _____

6. I fall from the sky. _____

Unit 11 Now try these   Focus on Word Work © Louis Fidge and Sarah Lindsay, HarperCollins*Publishers* 1998

Name _____

COPYMASTER
65

The word ending ed

1. Choose a word from the box to complete the sentence.

| packed   rocked   jumped   locked   helped |

a) Our teacher _helped_ us with the sums.

b) Tom _____ the baby to sleep.

c) Dad _____ the car door.

d) We _____ our suitcases.

e) Mohammed _____ over the log.

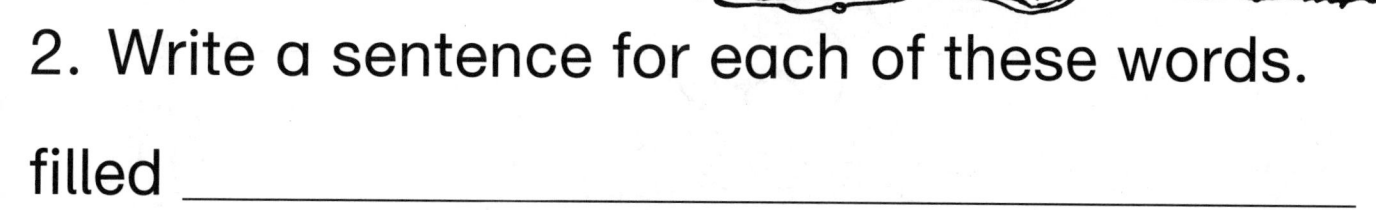

2. Write a sentence for each of these words.

filled _____

picked _____

Unit 12 Now try these   Focus on Word Work © Louis Fidge and Sarah Lindsay, HarperCollins*Publishers* 1998

Name _____

COPYMASTER 66

The word ending ing

What is Ben doing now?
Use the words in the box.

| reading | eating | kicking | talking |
| walking | licking | sleeping | jumping |

1. reading

2. _____

3. _____

4. _____

5. _____

6. _____

7. _____

8. _____

Unit 13 Now try these   *Focus on Word Work* © Louis Fidge and Sarah Lindsay, HarperCollins*Publishers* 1998

Name _____

COPYMASTER 67

Vowels and consonants

Sort the letters into the correct box.

q n b t
e z g
a y j s p
  l k h
r i   x d o
  c v m w f u

vowels   **consonants**

Unit 14 Now try these   *Focus on Word Work* © Louis Fidge and Sarah Lindsay, HarperCollins*Publishers* 1998

Name _____

COPYMASTER 68

ck

du**ck**   so**ck**

The letters **ck** are often at the end of words.

1. Match the words to the pictures.

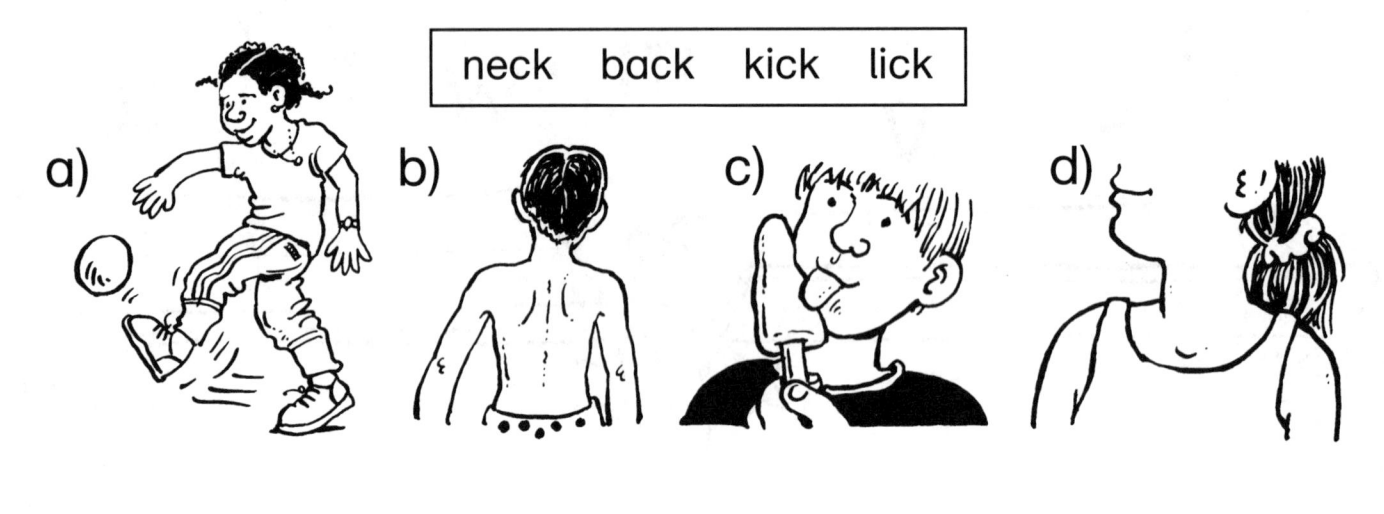

neck   back   kick   lick

a)   b)   c)   d)

_____   _____   _____   _____

2. Write three more words that end in **ck**.

_____   _____   _____

3. Choose two words ending in **ck** and use each of them in a sentence.

a) _____

b) _____

Focus on Word Work © Louis Fidge and Sarah Lindsay, Harper**Collins***Publishers* 1998

Name _____

COPYMASTER 69

ee and ea

bee

leaf

ee and **ea** often make the same sound.

1. Match the words to the pictures.

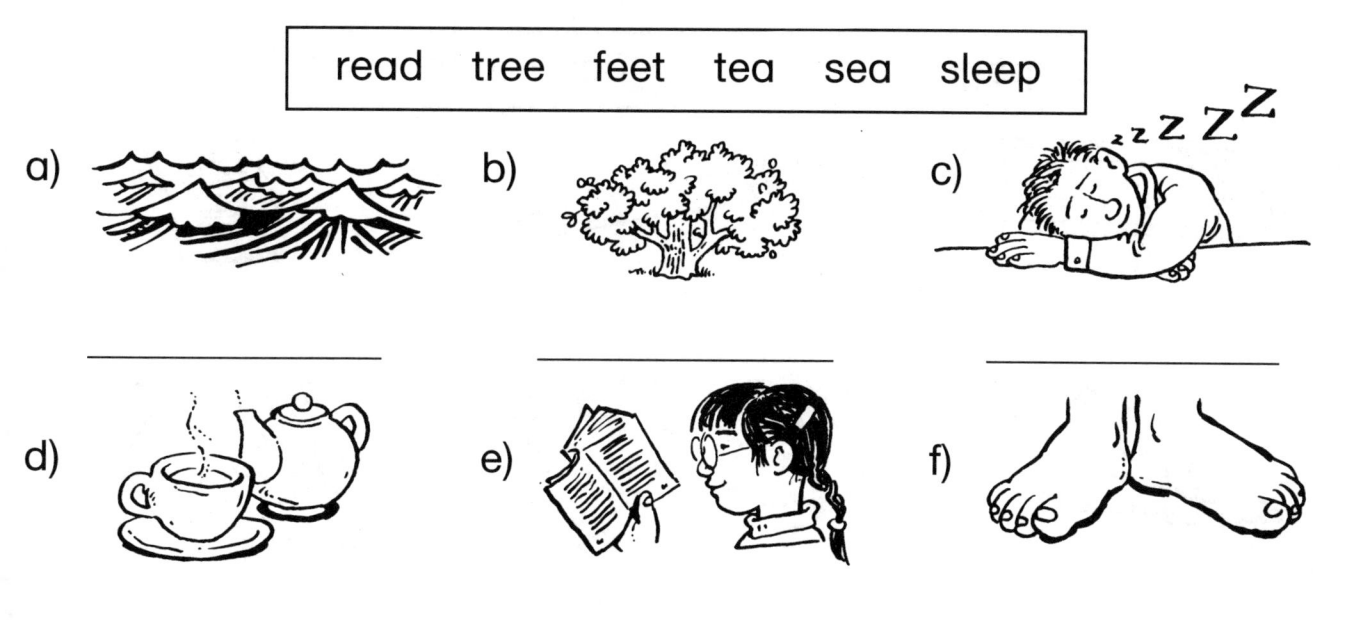

| read tree feet tea sea sleep |

a) _____   b) _____   c) _____

d) _____   e) _____   f) _____

2. Sort the **ee** and **ea** words into the boxes.

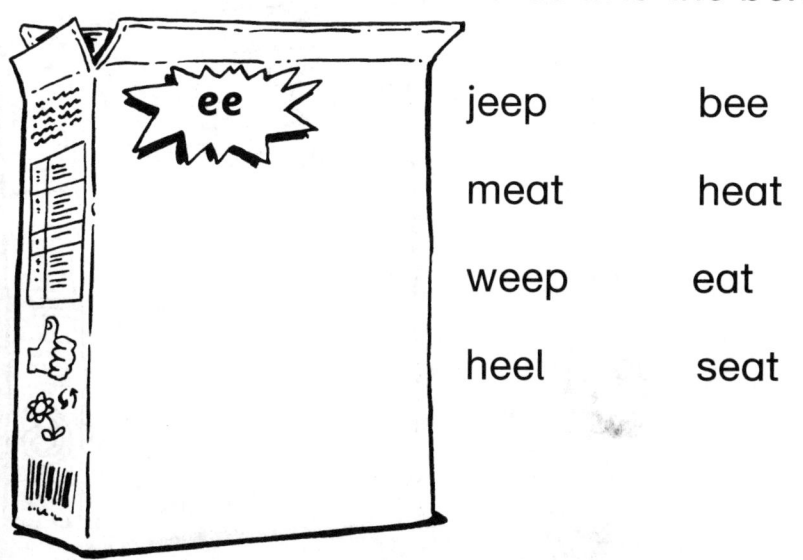

ee

jeep   bee

meat   heat

weep   eat

heel   seat

ea

Focus on Word Work © Louis Fidge and Sarah Lindsay, HarperCollinsPublishers 1998

Name _____

COPYMASTER
70

ai, ay and a-e

tail   hay    cage

ai, ay and **a-e** often make the same sound.

1. Match the words to the pictures.

| page | snail | tray | pay | race | nail |

a) 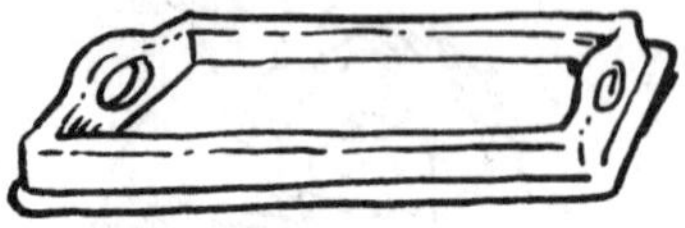 _____ b)  _____ c) _____

d)  _____ e)  _____ f) _____

2. Sort the **ai** and **ay** words into the boxes.

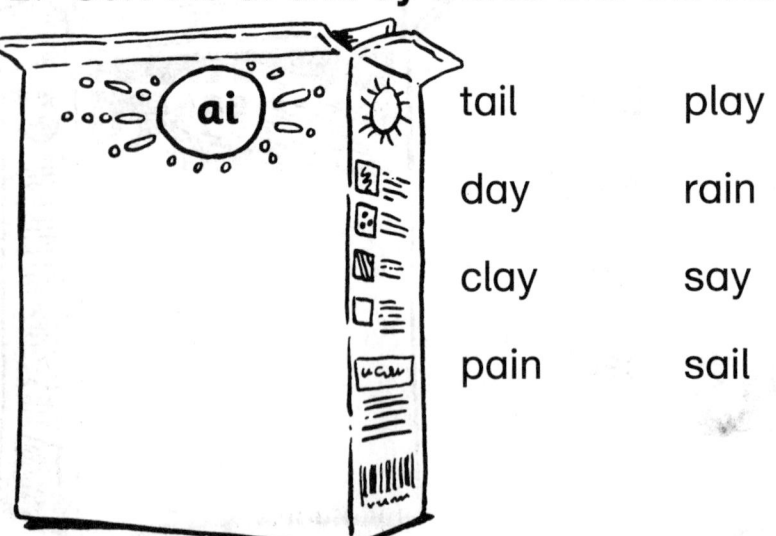

ai

tail   play
day   rain
clay   say
pain   sail

ay

Focus on Word Work © Louis Fidge and Sarah Lindsay, HarperCollins*Publishers* 1998

Name _____

COPYMASTER
71

ie, igh, i-e and y

tie   light   fly   kite

ie, igh, i-e and **y** often make the same sound.

1. Match the words to the pictures.

   pie   night   rice   fight   bike   cry

   a)   b)   c)

   d)   e)   f)

2. Sort the **ie** and **igh** words into the boxes.

   i-e

   kite   light
   bright five
   dive   like
   high   right

   igh

Focus on Word Work © Louis Fidge and Sarah Lindsay, HarperCollins*Publishers* 1998

Name _____

COPYMASTER 72

oa, ow and o-e

boat    bow    rose

oa, ow and o-e often make the same sound

1. Match the words to the pictures.

   | coat snow toad bone crow smoke |

   a)  _____   b)  _____   c) _____

   d)  _____   e)  _____   f) _____

2. Sort the **oa** and **o-e** words into the boxes.

   close   stone
   road   smoke
   coat   toad
   throne   goat

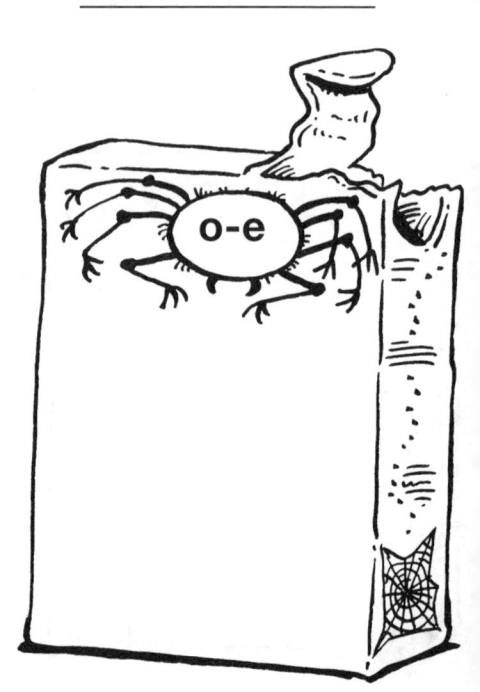

Focus on Word Work © Louis Fidge and Sarah Lindsay, HarperCollins*Publishers* 1998

Name _____

COPYMASTER
73

oo, ew, ue and u-e

m**oo**n   scr**ew**   gl**ue**   J**u**n**e**

oe, **ew**, **ue** and **u-e** often make the same sound.

1. Match the words to the pictures.

| spoon   tube   room   chew   glue   flute |

a)  _____   b)  _____   c) _____

d)  _____   e)  _____   f) _____

2. Sort the **oe** and **e-w** words into the boxes.

oo   **ew**

broom   tooth

chew   new

grew   room

goose   moon

Focus on Word Work © Louis Fidge and Sarah Lindsay, HarperCollins*Publishers* 1998

Name _____

COPYMASTER 74

Plural

Plural means more than one.

The **cat** sat on the mat.

The **<u>cats</u>** sat on the mat.

We add **s** to many words to show there is more than one.

1. Underline the **plural** word in each sentence.

    a) The dogs jumped in the mud!

    b) Sam put her pens in her bag.

    c) Amina ate four buns!

    d) Birds fly high in the sky.

    e) Five frogs live in the school pond.

2. Write three sentences. Each sentence must have a plural.

    a) _____

    b) _____

    c) _____

Focus on Word Work © Louis Fidge and Sarah Lindsay, HarperCollins*Publishers* 1998

Name _____

are and ere

Wh**ere** did we put the sp**are** key?

are and **ere** often make the same sound.

1. Underline the letters that make a similar sound to **are** in sp**are**.

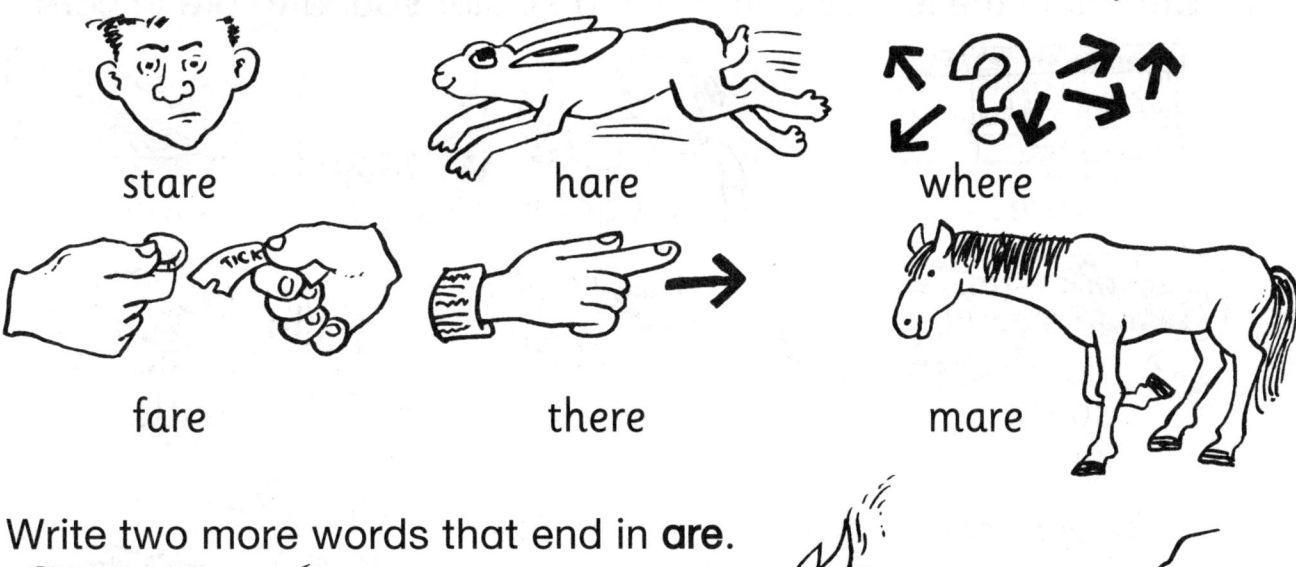

   stare   hare   where

   fare   there   mare

2. Write two more words that end in **are**.

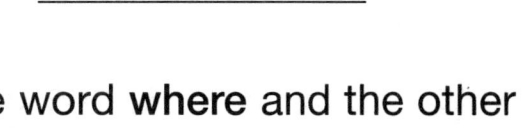

   _____   _____

3. Write two sentences, one using the word **where** and the other using the word **there**.

   a) _____

   b) _____

Focus on Word Work © Louis Fidge and Sarah Lindsay, HarperCollins*Publishers* 1998

Name _____

COPYMASTER
76

au and ore

The dog **cau**ght the apple c**ore**.

au and **ore** often make the same sound.

1. Underline the letters that make a similar sound to **ore** in c**ore**.

   store   daughter   shore

   sauce   score   author

2. Write two more words that end in **ore**.

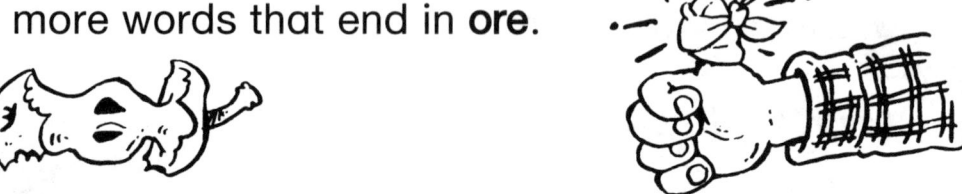

   _____   _____

3. Write two sentences, one using the word **August** and the other using the word **because**.

   a) _____

   b) _____

Focus on Word Work © Louis Fidge and Sarah Lindsay, HarperCollins*Publishers* 1998

Name _____

COPYMASTER
77

s**ch**ool   **ch**oir

Say these words aloud.
Listen to the sound the **ch** makes.

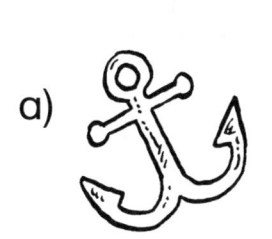

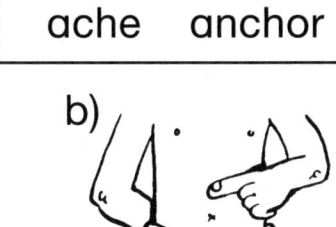

1. Match the words to the pictures.

   ache   anchor   chemist   stomach

   a)   b)   c)   d)

   _____ _____ _____ _____

2. Complete these words with **ch**.

   a __ __ e

   e __ __ o

3. Choose two words that contain **ch**. Use each of them in a sentence.

   a) _____

   b) _____

Focus on Word Work © Louis Fidge and Sarah Lindsay, HarperCollins*Publishers* 1998

Name _____

COPYMASTER 78

High frequency word checklist (Years 1/2)

about	after	again	an	another
as	back	ball	be	because
bed	been	boy	brother	but
by	call	came	can't	could
did	do	don't	dig	door
down	first	from	girl	good
got	had	half	has	have
help	her	here	him	his
home	house	how	if	jump
just	last	laugh	little	live
love	made	make	man	many
may	more	much	must	name
new	next	night	not	now
off	old	once	one	or
our	out	over	people	push
pull	put	ran	saw	school
seen	should	sister	so	some
take	than	that	their	them
then	there	these	three	time
too	took	tree	two	us
very	want	water	way	were
what	when	where	who	will
with	would	your		

Focus on Word Work © Louis Fidge and Sarah Lindsay, HarperCollins*Publishers* 1998

Name _____

COPYMASTER 79

High frequency words lotto cards

after	too	people	an	two
some	been	that	live	good
time	half	got	over	these

seen	much	her	laugh	made
just	should	people	half	because
here	night	many	house	time

must	another	school	would	sister
home	were	jump	came	again
don't	new	three	what	saw

Focus on Word Work © Louis Fidge and Sarah Lindsay, HarperCollins*Publishers* 1998

Name _____

COPYMASTER 80

High frequency words: lotto cards

ball	saw	water	than	has
don't	there	once	off	will
if	because	have	three	old

tree	put	man	door	as
would	not	his	took	home
by	push	our	first	way

then	make	can't	dig	their
now	boy	want	pull	call
brother	one	did	so	half

Focus on Word Work © Louis Fidge and Sarah Lindsay, HarperCollins*Publishers* 1998

Name _____

COPYMASTER
81

High frequency words: lotto cards

about	down	ran	where	school
jump	with	may	how	them
your	should	last	came	be

another	sister	when	more	help
back	who	little	do	out
take	love	him	could	again

next	were	from	new	or
girl	us	name	house	very
but	had	bed	what	night

Focus on Word Work © Louis Fidge and Sarah Lindsay, HarperCollins*Publishers* 1998

Name _____

High frequency words lotto cards

little	them	your	more	first
brother	where	seen	pull	how
will	good	could	do	bed

with	take	must	here	down
boy	want	out	love	from
if	some	tree	help	very

one	but	call	when	ran
made	just	dig	now	than
old	girl	live	got	can't

Focus on Word Work © Louis Fidge and Sarah Lindsay, HarperCollins*Publishers* 1998

Name _____

COPYMASTER
83

High frequency words game

Play the game.

Start • 1 • 2 • 3 • 4 • 5 • 6 • 7 • 8 • 9 • 10 • 11 • 12 • 13 • 14 • 15 • 16 • 17 • 18 • 19 • 20 • 21 • 22 • 23 • 24 • 25 • 26 • 27 • 28 • 29 • 30 • Finish

Focus on Word Work © Louis Fidge and Sarah Lindsay, HarperCollins*Publishers* 1998

Name _____

COPYMASTER 84

Writing high frequency words

Look at the word list.
Write four words that begin with each of these letters.

b _____ _____ _____ _____

c _____ _____ _____ _____

d _____ _____ _____ _____

h _____ _____ _____ _____

l _____ _____ _____ _____

n _____ _____ _____ _____

t _____ _____ _____ _____

w _____ _____ _____ _____

Focus on Word Work © Louis Fidge and Sarah Lindsay, HarperCollins*Publishers* 1998

Name _____

COPYMASTER
85

Writing high frequency words

Look at the word list.
Write six words that have two letters.

_____   _____   _____

_____   _____   _____

Write three words that begin with **ma**.

_____   _____   _____

Write three words that begin with **wh**.

_____   _____   _____

Write six words that begin with **th**.

_____   _____   _____

_____   _____   _____

Focus on Word Work © Louis Fidge and Sarah Lindsay, HarperCollins*Publishers* 1998

Name _____

High frequency words

COPYMASTER 86

Focus on Word Work © Louis Fidge and Sarah Lindsay, HarperCollins*Publishers* 1998

Name _____

COPYMASTER
87

Using high frequency words

We want **to** go in the tent.

Can we come **too**?

There is room for **two** more.

to   **too**   **two**

These words sound the same but are spelt differently, depending on how you use each word.

1. Add the correct **to**, **too** or **two** in the gaps.

a) "Can I have some more cake _____?"

b) James has _____ pet rabbits.

c) "Let's go _____ the park."

d) "We want _____ go on the train."

2. Write sentences using **to**, **too** or **two**.

a) _____

b) _____

c) _____

Focus on Word Work © Louis Fidge and Sarah Lindsay, HarperCollins*Publishers* 1998

COPYMASTER 88

Name _____

Using high frequency words

Can we go **there** on our holiday?

The children took **their** dog for a walk.

there   their

These words sound the same but are spelt differently, depending on how you use each word.

1. Add the correct **there** or **their** in the gaps.

a) Ben and Claire share _____ sweets.

b) _____ is a lot to do at the park.

c) In London, _____ is a palace.

d) Sadie and Anila got _____ clothes muddy.

e) The children collected _____ towels.

2. Write sentences using **there** or **their**.

a) _____

b) _____

c) _____

Focus on Word Work © Louis Fidge and Sarah Lindsay, HarperCollins*Publishers* 1998

Name _____

Year 1/2 Additional high frequency words

one	two	three	four
five	six	seven	eight
nine	ten	eleven	twelve
thirteen	fourteen	fifteen	sixteen
seventeen	eighteen	nineteen	twenty
Monday	Tuesday	Wednesday	Thursday
Friday	Saturday	Sunday	January
February	March	April	May
June	July	August	September
October	November	December	red
yellow	green	blue	white
black	orange	brown	pink

Focus on Word Work © Louis Fidge and Sarah Lindsay, HarperCollins*Publishers* 1998

Name _____

COPYMASTER 90

Additional high frequency words lotto cards

Monday	January	orange	Friday	twenty
December	sixteen	red	eight	June
ten	Sunday	thirteen	September	black

August	pink	nineteen	February	fourteen
white	Tuesday	six	eleven	yellow
April	seventeen	nine	November	Thursday

fifteen	four	October	green	March
seven	May	eighteen	twelve	Wednesday
Saturday	blue	five	brown	July

Focus on Word Work © Louis Fidge and Sarah Lindsay, HarperCollins*Publishers* 1998

Name _____

COPYMASTER 91

Additional words (1)

1. Each number in the picture is a colour.
Colour the picture.

one = **blue**   two = **green**   three = **orange**

four = **red**   five = **black**   six = **yellow**

2. Write the words for the colours you have used.

b_____   r_____   y_____

o_____   b_____   g_____

Focus on Word Work © Louis Fidge and Sarah Lindsay, Harper*Collins*Publishers 1998

Additional words (2)

Sunday • **Tuesday** • **Wednesday** • **Thursday** • **Monday** • **Friday** • **Saturday**

1. Look at the pictures. Fill the gaps.

   a) On _____ Jenny read her book.

   b) On _____ Jenny played with friends.

   c) On _____ Jenny went swimming.

   d) On _____ Jenny went to the fair.

   e) On _____ Jenny rode her bike.

   d) On _____ Jenny went shopping.

   e) On _____ Jenny walked the dog.

2. What did you do on Saturday? Write a sentence.

   _____

   _____